The Gita

The Greatness of the Sacred Hindu Text

Swami Vivekananda

Institute of Thought & Philosophy

GRAPEVINE INDIA

Published by

GRAPEVINE INDIA PUBLISHERS PVT LTD

www.grapevineindia.com
Delhi | Mumbai
email: grapevineindiapublishers@gmail.com

Ordering Information:
Quantity sales: Special discounts are available on quantity purchases by corporations, associations, and others. For details, reach out to the publisher.

First published by Grapevine India 2023

The mission of the Institute of Thought and Philosophy is to preserve and propagate the teachings of Swami Vivekananda. This great Indian spiritual leader is known for introducing the West to Hinduism. Drawing from his vast literary legacy, we provide valuable insights and practical guidance for modern living.

Have any query or feedback? Please reach out to us at ITPPress123@gmail.com

An Introduction to the Gita

To understand the Gita requires its historical background. The Gita is a commentary on the Upanishads. The Upanishads are the Bible of India. They occupy the same place as the New Testament does. There are more than a hundred books comprising the Upanishads, some very small and some big, each a separate treatise.

The Upanishads do not reveal the life of any teacher, but simply teach principles. They are as it were shorthand notes taken down of discussion in learned assemblies, generally in the courts of kings. The word Upanishad may mean "sittings" or "sitting near a teacher".

Those of you who may have studied some of the Upanishads can understand how they are condensed shorthand sketches. After long discussions had been held, they were taken down, possibly from memory.

The difficulty is that you get very little of the background. Only the luminous points are mentioned there. The origin of ancient Sanskrit is 5000 B.C.; the Upanishads are at least two thousand years before that. Nobody knows exactly how old they are.

The Gita takes the ideas of the Upanishads and in some cases the very words. They are strung together with the idea of bringing out, in a compact, condensed, and systematic form, the whole subject the Upanishads deal with.

The original scriptures of the Hindus are called the Vedas. They were so vast — the mass of writings — that if the texts alone were brought here, this room would not contain them. Many of them are lost. They were divided into branches, each branch put into the head of certain priests and kept alive by memory.

Such men still exist. They will repeat book after book of the Vedas without missing a single intonation.

The larger portion of the Vedas has disappeared. The small portion left makes a whole library by itself. The oldest of these contains the hymns of the Rig-Veda. It is the aim of the modern scholar to restore the sequence of the Vedic compositions.

The old, orthodox idea is quite different, as your orthodox idea of the Bible is quite different from the modern scholar's. The Vedas are divided into two portions: one the Upanishads, the philosophical portion, the other the work portion.

We will try to give a little idea of the work portion. It consists of rituals and hymns, various hymns addressed to various gods. The ritual portion is composed of ceremonies, some of them very elaborate. A great many priests are required. The priestly function became a science by itself, owing to the elaboration of the ceremonials.

Gradually the popular idea of veneration grew round

these hymns and rituals. The gods disappeared and in their place were left the rituals.

That was the curious development in India. The orthodox Hindu the Mimamsaka does not believe in gods, the unorthodox believe in them. If you ask the orthodox Hindu what the meaning is of these gods in the Vedas, he will not be able to give any satisfactory answer. The priests sing these hymns and pour libations and offering into the fire. When you ask the orthodox Hindu the meaning of this, he says that words have the power to produce certain effects.

That is all. There is all the natural and supernatural power that ever existed. The Vedas are simply words that have the mystical power to produce effects if the sound intonation is right. If one sound is wrong it will not do. Each one must be perfect. Thus what in other religions is called prayer disappeared and the Vedas became the gods.

So you see the tremendous importance that was attached to the words of the Vedas. These are the eternal words out of which the whole universe has been produced. There cannot be any thought without the word.

Thus whatever there is in this world is the manifestation of thought, and thought can only manifest itself through words. This mass of words by which the unmanifested thought becomes manifest, that is what is meant by the Vedas.

It follows that the external existence of everything depends on the Vedas, for thought does not exist without the word. If the word "horsc" did not exist, none could think of a horse. So there must be an intimate relation between thought, word, and the external object.

What are these words in reality? The Vedas. They do not call it Sanskrit language at all. It is Vedic language, a divine language. Sanskrit is a degenerate form. So are all other languages. There is no language older than Vedic.

You may ask, "Who wrote the Vedas?" They were not written. The words are the Vedas. A word is Veda, if I can pronounce it rightly. Then it will immediately produce the desired effect.

This mass of Vedas eternally exists and all the world is the manifestation of this mass of words. Then when the cycle ends, all this manifestation of energy becomes finer and finer, becomes only words, then thought. In the next cycle, first the thought changes into words and then out of those words the whole universe is produced. If there is something here that is not in the Vedas, that is your delusion. It does not exist.

Numerous books upon that subject alone defend the Vedas. If you tell their authors that the Vedas must have been pronounced by men first, they will simply laugh. You never heard of any man uttering them for the first time.

Take Buddha's words. There is a tradition that he

lived and spoke these words many times before. If the Christian stands up and says, "My religion is a historical religion and therefore yours is wrong and ours is true," the Mimamsaka replies, "Yours being historical, you confess that a man invented it nineteen hundred years ago. That which is true must be infinite and eternal. That is the one test of truth. It never decays, it is always the same. You confess your religion was created by such-and-such a man. The Vedas were not. By no prophets or anything. Only infinite words, infinite by their very nature, from which the whole universe comes and goes."

In the abstract it is perfectly correct. The sound must be the beginning of creation. There must be germ sounds like germ plasm. There cannot be any ideas without the words. Wherever there are sensations, ideas, emotions, there must be words.

The difficulty is when they say that these four books are the Vedas and nothing else. Then the Buddhist will stand up and say, "Ours are Vedas. They were revealed to us later on." That cannot be. Nature does not go on in that way. Nature does not manifest her laws bit by bit, an inch of gravitation today and another inch tomorrow.

No, every law is complete. There is no evolution in law at all. It is given once and for ever. It is all nonsense, this "new religion and better inspiration," and all that. It means nothing. There may be a hundred thousand laws and man may know only a few today. We discover them — that is all.

Those old priests with their tremendous claims about eternal words, having dethroned the gods, took the place of the gods. Thcy said, "You do not understand the power of words. We know how to use them. We are the living gods of the world. Pay us; we will manipulate the words, and you will get what you want. Can you pronounce the words yourself? You cannot, for, mind you, one mistake will produce the opposite effect. You want to be rich, handsome, have a long life, a fine husband?" Only pay the priest and keep quiet!

Yet there is another side. The ideal of the first part of the Vedas is entirely different from the ideal of the other part, the Upanishads. The ideal of the first part coincides with that of all other religions of the world except the Vedanta. The ideal is enjoyment here and hereafter — man and wife, husband and children. Pay your dollar, and the priest will give you a certificate, and you will have a happy time afterwards in heaven.

You will find all your people there and have this merry-go-round without end. No tears, no weeping — only laughing. No stomach-ache, but yet eating. No headache, but yet parties. That, considered the priests, was the highest goal of man.

There is another idea in this philosophy which is according to your modern ideas. Man is a slave of nature, and slave eternally he has got to remain. We call it Karma. Karma means law, and it applies everywhere. Everything is bound by Karma.

"Is there no way out?" "No! Remain slaves all through the years — fine slaves. We will manipulate the words so that you will only have the good and not the bad side of all — if you will pay us enough."

That was the ideal of the Mimamsakas. These are the ideals which are popular throughout the ages. The vast mass of mankind are never thinkers. Even if they try to think, the effect of the vast mass of superstitions on them is terrible. The moment they weaken, one blow comes, and the backbone breaks into twenty pieces.

They can only be moved by lures and threats. They can never move of their own accord. They must be frightened, horrified, or terrorised, and they are your slaves for ever. They have nothing else to do but to pay and obey. Everything else is done by the priest.

How much easier religion becomes! You see, you have nothing to do. Go home and sit quietly. Somebody is doing the whole thing for you. Poor, poor animals!

Side by side, there was the other system. The Upanishads are diametrically opposite in all their conclusions. First of all, the Upanishads believe in God, the creator of the universe, its ruler. You find later on the idea of a benign Providence. It is an entirely opposite conception. Now, although we hear the priest, the ideal is much more subtle. Instead of many gods they made one God.

The second idea, that you are all bound by the law of

Karma, the Upanishads admit, but they declare the way out. The goal of man is to go beyond law. And enjoyment can never be the goal, because enjoyment can only be in nature.

In the third place, the Upanishads condemn all the sacrifices and say that is mummery. That may give you all you want, but it is not desirable, for the more you get, the more you want, and you run round and round in a circle eternally, never getting to the end — enjoying and weeping. Such a thing as eternal happiness is impossible anywhere. It is only a child's dream. The same energy becomes joy and sorrow.

I have changed my psychology a bit today. I have found the most curious fact. You have a certain idea and you do not want to have it, and you think of something else, and the idea you want to suppress is entirely suppressed. What is that idea? I saw it come out in fifteen minutes. It came out and staggered me. It was strong, and it came in such a violent and terrible fashion that I thought here was a madman. And when it was over, all that had happened was a suppression of the previous emotion.

What came out? It was my own bad impression which had to be worked out. "Nature will have her way. What can suppression do?" (Gita, III. 33.) That is a terrible statement in the Gita. It seems it may be a vain struggle after all. You may have a hundred thousand urges competing at the same time. You may repress them, but the moment the spring rebounds, the whole thing is there again.

But there is hope. If you are powerful enough, you can divide your consciousness into twenty parts all at the same time. I am changing my psychology. Mind grows. That is what the Yogis say. There is one passion and it rouses another, and the first one dies. If you are angry, and then happy, the next moment the anger passes away. Out of that anger you manufactured the next state.

These states are always interchangeable. Eternal happiness and misery are a child's dream. The Upanishads point out that the goal of man is neither misery nor happiness, but we have to be master of that out of which these are manufactured. We must be masters of the situation at its very root, as it were.

The other point of divergence is: the Upanishads condemn all rituals, especially those that involve the killing of animals. They declare those all nonsense. One school of old philosophers says that you must kill such an animal at a certain time if the effect is to be produced.

You may reply, "But there is also the sin of taking the life of the animal; you will have to suffer for that." They say that is all nonsense. How do you know what is right and what is wrong? Your mind says so? Who cares what your mind says? What nonsense are you talking? You are setting your mind against the scriptures.

If your mind says something and the Vedas say something else, stop your mind and believe in the

Vedas. If they say, killing a man is right, that is right. If you say, "No, my conscience says otherwise," it won't do. Thc moment you believe in any book as the eternal word, as sacred, no more can you question.

I do not see how you people here believe in the Bible whenever you say about it, "How wonderful those words are, how right and how good!" Because, if you believe in the Bible as the word of God, you have no right to judge at all. The moment you judge, you think you are higher than the Bible. Then what is the use of the Bible to you?

The priests say, "We refuse to make the comparison with your Bible or anybody's. It is no use comparing, because — what is the authority? There it ends. If you think something is not right, go and get it right according to the Vedas."

The Upanishads believe in that, but they have a higher standard too. On the one hand, they do not want to overthrow the Vedas, and on the other they see these animal sacrifices and the priests stealing everybody's money. But in the psychology they are all alike. All the differences have been in the philosophy, regarding the nature of the soul.

Has it a body and a mind? And is the mind only a bundle of nerves, the motor nerves and the sensory nerves? Psychology, they all take for granted, is a perfect science. There cannot be any difference there. All the fight has been regarding philosophy — the nature of the soul, and God, and all that.

Then another great difference between the priests and the Upanishads. The Upanishads say, renounce. That is the test of everything. Renounce everything. It is the creative faculty that brings us into all this entanglement. The mind is in its own nature when it is calm. The moment you can calm it, that very moment you will know the truth.

What is it that is whirling the mind? Imagination, creative activity. Stop creation and you know the truth. All power of creation must stop, and then you know the truth at once.

On the other hand, the priests are all for creation. Imagine a species of life in which there is no creative activity. It is unthinkable. The people had to have a plan of evolving a stable society. A system of rigid selection was adopted. For instance, no people who are blind and halt can be married.

As a result you will find so much less deformity in India than in any other country in the world. Epileptics and insane people are very rare there. That is owing to direct selection.

The priests say, "Let them become Sannyasins." On the other hand, the Upanishads say, "Oh no, the earth's best and finest and freshest flowers should be laid upon the altar. The strong, the young, with sound intellect and sound body — they must struggle for the truth."

So with all these divergences of opinion, I have told you that the priests already differentiated themselves into a separate caste. The second is the caste of the kings. All the Upanishadic philosophy is from the brains of kings, not priests.

There runs an economic struggle through every religious struggle. This animal called man has some religious influence, but he is guided by economy. Individuals are guided by something else, but the mass of mankind never made a move unless economy was involved. You may preach a religion that may not be perfect in every detail, but if there is an economic background to it, and you have the most ardent champions to preach it, you can convince a whole country.

Whenever any religion succeeds, it must have economic value. Thousands of similar sects will be struggling for power, but only those who meet the real economic problem will have it.

Man is guided by the stomach. He walks and the stomach goes first and the head afterwards. Have you not seen that? It will take ages for the head to go first. By the time a man is sixty years of age, he is called out of the world. The whole of life is one delusion, and just when you begin to see things the way they are, you are snatched off.

So long as the stomach went first you were all right. When children's dreams begin to vanish and you begin to look at things the way they are, the head goes. Just when the head goes first, you go out.

For the religion of the Upanishads to be popularised was a hard task. Very little economy is there, but tremendous altruism.

The Upanishads had very little kingdom, although they were discovered by kings that held all the royal power in their hands. So the struggle began to be fiercer. Its culminating point came two thousand years after, in Buddhism.

The seed of Buddhism is here, in the ordinary struggle between the king and the priest; and in the struggle all religion declined. One wanted to sacrifice religion, the other wanted to cling to the sacrifices, to Vedic gods, etc. Buddhism broke the chains of the masses. All castes and creeds alike became equal in a minute. So the great religious ideas in India exist, but have yet to be preached: otherwise they do no good.

In every country it is the priest who is conservative, for two reasons — because it is his bread and because he can only move with the people. All priests are not strong. If the people say, "Preach two thousand gods," the priests will do it. They are the servants of the congregation who pay them. God does not pay them.

So blame yourselves before blaming the priests. You can only get the government and the religion and the priesthood you deserve, and no better.

So the great struggle began in India and it comes to one of its culminating points in the Gita. When it was causing fear that all India was going to be broken up between the two groups, there rose this man Krishna, and in the Gita he tries to reconcile the ceremony and the philosophy of the priests and the people.

Krishna is loved and worshipped in the same way as you do Christ. The difference is only in the age. The Hindus keep the birthday of Krishna as you do Christ's. Krishna lived five thousand years ago and his life is full of miracles, some of them very similar to those in the life of Christ.

The child was born in prison. The father took him away and put him with the shepherds. All children born in that year were ordered to be killed. He was killed; that was his fate.

Krishna was a married man. There are thousands of books about him. They do not interest me much. The Hindus are great in telling stories, you see. If the Christian missionaries tell one story from their Bible, the Hindus will produce twenty stories.

You say the whale swallowed Jonah; the Hindus say someone swallowed an elephant. Since I was a child

I have heard about Krishna's life. I take it for granted there must have been a man called Krishna, and his Gita shows he has left a wonderful book.

I told you, you can understand the character of a man by analysing the fables about him. The fables have the nature of decorations. You must find they are all polished and manipulated to fit into the character.

For instance, take Buddha. The central idea is sacrifice. There are thousands of folklore, but in every case the sacrifice must have been kept up. There are thousands of stories about Lincoln, about some characteristic of that great man. You take all the fables and find the general idea and know that that was the central character of the man.

You find in Krishna that non-attachment is the central idea. He does not need anything. He does not want anything. He works for work's sake. "Work for work's sake. Worship for worship's sake. Do good because it is good to do good. Ask no more." That must have been the character of the man. Otherwise these fables could not be brought down to the one idea of non-attachment. The Gita is not his only sermon.

He is the most rounded man I know of, wonderfully developed equally in brain and heart and hand. Every moment of his is alive with activity, either as a gentleman, warrior, minister, or something else. Great as a gentleman, as a scholar, as a poet. This all-rounded and wonderful activity and combination of brain and heart you see in the Gita and other books. Most wonderful heart, exquisite language, and nothing can approach it anywhere.

This tremendous activity of the man — the impression is still there. Five thousand years have passed and he has influenced millions and millions. Just think what an influence this man has over the whole world, whether you know it or not. My regard for him is for his perfect sanity. No cobwebs in that brain, no superstition. He knows the use of everything, and when it is necessary to assign a place to each, he is there.

Those that talk, go everywhere, question about the mystery of the Vedas, etc., they do not know the truth. They are no better than frauds. There is a place in the Vedas even for superstition, for ignorance. The whole secret is to find out the proper place for everything.

Then that heart! He is the first man, way before Buddha, to open the door of religion to every caste. That wonderful mind! That tremendously active life! Buddha's activity was on one plane, the plane of teaching. He could not keep his wife and child and become a teacher at the same time. Krishna preached in the midst of the battlefield.

"He who in the midst of intense activity finds himself in the greatest calmness, and in the greatest peace finds intense activity, that is the greatest Yogi as well as the wisest man." (Ibid. IV. 18.) It means nothing to this man — the flying of missiles about him. Calm and sedate he goes on discussing the problems of life and death. Each one of the prophets is the best commentary on his own teaching.

If you want to know what is meant by the doctrine of the New Testament, you go to Mr. So-and-so. But read again and again the four Gospels and try to understand their import in the light of the wonderful life of the Master as depicted there. The great men think, and you and I also think.

But there is a difference. We think and our bodies do not follow. Our actions do not harmonise with our thoughts. Our words have not the power of the words that become Vedas. Whatever they think must be accomplished. If they say, "I do this," the body does it. Perfect obedience. This is the end. You can think yourself God in one minute, but you cannot be God. That is the difficulty. They become what they think. We will become only by degrees.

You see, that was about Krishna and his time. In the next lecture we will know more of his book.

An Aid to Understanding the Gita

The book known as the Gita forms a part of the Mahabharata. Now it is for us to see what there is in the Gita. If we study thc Upanishads we notice, in wandering through the mazes of many irrelevant subjects, the sudden introduction of the discussion of a great truth, just as in the midst of a huge wilderness a traveller unexpectedly comes across here and there an exquisitely beautiful rose, with its leaves, thorns, roots, all entangled.

Compared with that, the Gita is like these truths beautifully arranged together in their proper places — like a fine garland or a bouquet of the choicest flowers. The Upanishads deal elaborately with Shraddha in many places, but hardly mention Bhakti. In the Gita, on the other hand, the subject of Bhakti is not only again and again dealt with, but in it, the innate spirit of Bhakti has attained its culmination.

Now in the first place, let us see what grounds there are for such inquiry. We know that there were many who went by the name of Veda-Vyasa; and among them who was the real author of the Gita — the Badarayana Vyasa or Dvaipayana Vyasa?

"Vyasa" was only a title. Anyone who composed a new Purana was known by the name of Vyasa, like the word Vikramaditya, which was also a general name.

Another point is, the book, Gita, had not been much known to the generality of people before Shankaracharya made it famous by writing his great commentary on it. Long before that, there was current, according to many, the commentary on it by Bodhayana.

Then as to the second point in question, much doubt exists about the personality of Krishna.

In one place in the Chhandogya Upanishad we find mention of Krishna, the son of Devaki, who received spiritual instructions from one Ghora, a Yogi. In the Mahabharata, Krishna is the king of Dwaraka; and in the Vishnu Purana we find a description of Krishna playing with the Gopis.

In ancient times there was very little tendency in our country to find out truths by historical research. So any one could say what he thought best without substantiating it with proper facts and evidence. Another thing: in those ancient times there was very little hankering after name and fame in men. So it often happened that one man composed a book and made it pass current in the name of his Guru or of someone else.

In such cases it is very hazardous for the investigator of historical facts to get at the truth. In ancient times they had no knowledge whatever of geography; imagination ran riot. And so we meet with such fantastic creations of the brain as sweet-ocean, milk-ocean, clarified-butter-ocean, curd-ocean, etc! In the Puranas, we find one living ten thousand years, another a hundred thousand years!

But the Vedas say, — "Man lives a hundred years." Whom shall we follow here? So, to reach a correct conclusion in the case of Krishna is well-nigh impossible.

It is human nature to build round the real character of a great man all sorts of imaginary superhuman attributes. As regards Krishna the same must have happened, but it seems quite probable that he was a king. Quite probable I say, because in ancient times in our country it was chiefly the kings who exerted themselves most in the preaching of Brahma-Jnana.

Another point to be especially noted here is that whoever might have been the author of the Gita, we find its teachings the same as those in the whole of the Mahabharata. From this we can safely infer that in the age of the Mahabharata some great man arose and preached the Brahma-Jnana in this new garb to the then existing society.

Another fact comes to the fore that in the olden days, as one sect after another arose, there also came into existence and use among them one new scripture or another. It happened, too, that in the lapse of time both the sect and its scripture died out, or the sect ceased to exist but its scripture remained.

Similarly, it was quite probable that the Gita was the scripture of such a sect which had embodied its high and noble ideas in this sacred book.

Now to the third point, bearing on the subject of the Kurukshetra War, no special evidence in support of it can be adduced. But there is no doubt that there was a war fought between the Kurus and the Panchalas.

Another thing: how could there be so much discussion about Jnana, Bhakti, and Yoga on the battle-field, where the huge army stood in battle array ready to fight, just waiting for the last signal? And was any shorthand writer present there to note down every word spoken between Krishna and Arjuna, in the din and turmoil of the battle-field? According to some, this Kurukshetra War is only an allegory.

When we sum up its esoteric significance, it means the war which is constantly going on within man between the tendencies of good and evil. This meaning, too, may not be irrational.

About the fourth point, there is enough ground of doubt as regards the historicity of Arjuna and others, and it is this: Shatapatha Brahmana is a very ancient book. In it are mentioned somewhere all the names of those who were the performers of the Ashvamedha Yajna: but in those places there is not only no mention, but no hint even of the names of Arjuna and others, though it speaks of Janamejaya, the son of Parikshit who was a grandson of Arjuna. Yet in the Mahabharata and other books it is stated that Yudhishthira, Arjuna, and others celebrated the Ashvamedha sacrifice.

One thing should be especially remembered here, that there is no connection between these historical researches and our real aim, which is the knowledge that leads to the acquirement of Dharma. Even if the historicity of the whole thing is proved to be absolutely false today, it will not in the least be any loss to us.

Then what is the use of so much historical research, you may ask. It has its use, because we have to get at the truth; it will not do for us to remain bound by wrong ideas born of ignorance. In this country people think very little of the importance of such inquiries. Many of the sects believe that in order to preach a good thing which may be beneficial to many, there is no harm in telling an untruth, if that helps such preaching, or in other words, the end justifies the means.

Hence we find many of our Tantras beginning with, "Mahadeva said to Parvati". But our duty should be to convince ourselves of the truth, to believe in truth only. Such is the power of superstition, or faith in old traditions without inquiry into its truth, that it keeps men bound hand and foot, so much so, that even Jesus the Christ, Mohammed, and other great men believed in many such superstitions and could not shake them off. You have to keep your eye always fixed on truth only and shun all superstitions completely.

Arjuna and Krishna

The Gita requires a little preliminary introduction. The scene is laid on the battlefield of Kurukshetra. There were two branches of the same race fighting for the empire of India about five thousand years ago. The Pandavas had the right, but the Kauravas had the might. The Pandavas were five brothers, and they were living in a forest. Krishna was the friend of the Pandavas. The Kauravas would not grant them as much land as would cover the point of a needle.

The opening scene is the battlefield, and both sides see their relatives and friends — one brother on one side and another on the other side; a grandfather on one side, grandson on the other side. When Arjuna sees his own friends and relatives on the other side and knows that he may have to kill them, his heart gives way and he says that he will not fight. Thus begins the Gita.

For all of us in this world life is a continuous fight. Many a time comes when we want to interpret our weakness and cowardice as forgiveness and renunciation. There is no merit in the renunciation of a beggar. If a person who can give a blow forbears, there is merit in that. If a person who has, gives up, there is merit in that. We know how often in our lives through laziness and cowardice we give up the battle and try to hypnotise our minds into the belief that we are brave.

The Gita opens with this very significant verse: "Arise, O Prince! Give up this faint-heartedness, this weakness! Stand up and fight!" (Gita, II. 3.) Then Arjuna, trying to argue the matter with Krishna, brings higher moral ideas, how non-resistance is better than resistance, and so on. He is trying to justify himself, but he cannot fool Krishna. Krishna is the higher Self, or God. He sees through the argument at once. In this case the motive is weakness. Arjuna sees his own relatives and he cannot strike them.

There is a conflict in Arjuna's heart between his emotionalism and his duty. The nearer we are to beasts and birds, the more we are in the hells of emotion. We call it love. It is self-hypnotisation. We are under the control of our emotions like animals. A cow can sacrifice its life for its young. Every animal can.

What of that? It is not the blind, birdlike emotion that leads to perfection. To reach the eternal consciousness, that is the goal of man! There emotion has no place, nor sentimentalism, nor anything that belongs to the senses — only the light of pure reason. There man stands as spirit.

Now, Arjuna is under the control of this emotionalism. He is not what he should be — a great self-controlled, enlightened sage working through the eternal light of reason. He has become like an animal, like a baby, just letting his heart carry away his brain, making a fool of himself and trying to cover his weakness with the flowery names of "love" and so on.

Krishna sees through that. Arjuna talks like a man of little learning and brings out many reasons, but at the same time he talks the language of a fool.

“The sage is not sorry for those that are living nor for those that die.” (Ibid. 11.) Krishna says: “You cannot die nor can I. There was never a time when we did not exist. There will never be a time when we shall not exist. As in this life a man begins with childhood, and passes through youth and old age, so at death he merely passes into another kind of body. Why should a wise man be sorry?” (Ibid. 12-13.)

And where is the beginning of this emotionalism that has got hold of you? It is in the senses. “It is the touch of the senses that brings all this quality of existence: heat and cold, pleasure and pain. They come and go.” (Ibid. 14.) Man is miserable this moment, happy the next. As such he cannot experience the nature of the soul.

“Existence can never be non-existence, neither can non-existence ever become existence. Know, therefore, that that which pervades all this universe is without beginning or end. It is unchangeable. There is nothing in the universe that can change the Changeless. Though this body has its beginning and end, the dweller in the body is infinite and without end.” (Ibid. 16-18.)

Knowing this, stand up and fight! Not one step back, that is the idea. Fight it out, whatever comes. Let the stars move from the sphere! Let the whole world stand against us! Death means only a change of garment.

What of it? Thus fight! You gain nothing by becoming cowards. Taking a step backward, you do not avoid any misfortunc. You have cried to all the gods in the world. Has misery ceased? The masses in India cry to sixty million gods, and still die like dogs. Where are these gods? The gods come to help you when you have succeeded. So what is the use? Die game.

This bending the knee to superstitions, this selling yourself to your own mind does not befit you, my soul. You are infinite, deathless, birthless. Because you are infinite spirit, it does not befit you to be a slave. Arise! Awake! Stand up and fight! Die if you must. There is none to help you. You are all the world. Who can help you?

"Beings are unknown to our human senses before birth and after death. It is only in the interim that they are manifest. What is there to grieve about? (Ibid. 28.)

"Some look at It the Self with wonder. Some talk of It as wonderful. Others hear of It as wonderful. Others, hearing of It, do not understand." (Ibid. 29.)

But if you say that killing all these people is sinful, then consider this from the standpoint of your own caste-duty. "Making pleasure and misery the same, making success and defeat the same, do thou stand up and fight. (Ibid. 38.)

This is the beginning of another peculiar doctrine of the

Gita — the doctrine of non-attachment. That is to say, we have to bear the result of our own actions because we attach ourselves to them. "Only what is done as duty for duty's sake can scatter the bondage of Karma." (Ibid. 39.) There is no danger that you can overdo it. "If you do even a little of it, this Yoga will save you from the terrible round of birth and death. (Ibid. 40.)

"Know, Arjuna, the mind that succeeds is the mind that is concentrated. The minds that are taken up with two thousand subjects (have) their energies dispersed. Some can talk flowery language and think there is nothing beyond the Vedas. They want to go to heaven. They want good things through the power of the Vedas, and so they make sacrifices." (Ibid. 41-43.) Such will never attain any success in spiritual life unless they give up all these materialistic ideas. (Ibid. 44.)

That is another great lesson. Spirituality can never be attained unless all material ideas are given up. What is in the senses? The senses are all delusion. People wish to retain them in heaven even after they are dead — a pair of eyes, a nose. Some imagine they will have more organs than they have now. They want to see God sitting on a throne through all eternity — the material body of God.

Such men's desires are for the body, for food and drink and enjoyment. It is the materialistic life prolonged. Man cannot think of anything beyond this life. This life is all for the body. "Such a man never comes to that concentration which leads to freedom." (Ibid. 44.)

"The Vedas only teach things belonging to the three Gunas, to Sattva, Rajas, and Tamas." (Ibid. 45.) The Vedas only teach about things in nature. People cannot think anything they do not see on earth. If they talk about heaven, they think of a king sitting on a throne, of people burning incense. It is all nature, nothing beyond nature. The Vedas, therefore, teach nothing but nature. "Go beyond nature, beyond the dualities of existence, beyond your own consciousness, caring for nothing, neither for good nor for evil." (Ibid. 45.)

We have identified ourselves with our bodies. We are only body, or rather, possessed of a body. If I am pinched, I cry. All this is nonsense, since I am the soul. All this chain of misery, imagination, animals, gods, and demons, everything, the whole world all this comes from the identification of ourselves with the body. I am spirit.

Why do I jump if you pinch me? Look at the slavery of it. Are you not ashamed? We are religious! We are philosophers! We are sages! Lord bless us! What are we? Living hells, that is what we are. Lunatics, that is what we are!

We cannot give up the idea of body. We are earth-bound. Our ideas are burial grounds. When we leave the body we are bound by thousands of elements to those ideas.

Who can work without any attachment? That is the real question. Such a man is the same whether his work succeeds or fails. His heart does not give one false beat even if his whole life-work is burnt to ashes in a moment. "This is the sage who always works for work's sake without caring for the results.

Thus he goes beyond the pain of birth and death. Thus he becomes free." (Ibid. 51.) Then he sees that this attachment is all delusion. The Self can never be attached.

Then he goes beyond all the scriptures and philosophies. (Ibid. 52.) If the mind is deluded and pulled into a whirlpool by books and scriptures, what is the good of all these scriptures? One says this, another says that. What book shall you take? Stand alone! See the glory of your own soul, and see that you will have to work. Then you will become a man of firm will. (Ibid. 53.)

Arjuna asks: "Who is a person of established will?" (Ibid. 54.)

Krishna answers: "The man who has given up all desires, who desires nothing, not even this life, nor freedom, nor gods, nor work, nor anything. When he has become perfectly satisfied, he has no more cravings." (Ibid. 55.) He has seen the glory of the Self and has found that the world, and the gods, and heaven are within his own Self.

Then the gods become no gods; death becomes no death; life becomes no life. Everything has changed.

"A man is said to be illumined if his will has become firm, if his mind is not disturbed by misery, if he does not desire any happiness, if he is free of all attachment, of all fear, of all anger. (Ibid. 56.)

"As the tortoise can draw in his legs, and if you strike him, not one foot comes out, even so the sage can draw all his sense-organs inside," (Ibid. 58.) and nothing can force them out. Nothing can shake him, no temptation or anything. Let the universe tumble about him, it does not make one single ripple in his mind.

Then comes a very important question. Sometimes people fast for days. When the worst man has fasted for twenty days, he becomes quite gentle. Fasting and torturing themselves have been practiced by people all over the world.

Krishna's idea is that this is all nonsense. He says that the senses will for the moment recede from the man who tortures himself, but will emerge again with twenty times more power. What should you do? The idea is to be natural — no asceticism. Go on, work, only mind that you are not attached. The will can never be fixed strongly in the man who has not learnt and practiced the secret of non-attachment.

I go out and open my eyes. If something is there, I must see it. I cannot help it. The mind runs after the senses. Now the senses must give up any reaction to nature.

"Where it is dark night for the sense-bound world, the

self controlled man is awake. It is daylight for him. And where the world is awake, the sage sleeps." (Ibid. 69.)

Where is the world awake? In the senses. People want to eat and drink and have children, and then they die a dog's death. They are always awake for the senses. Even their religion is just for that. They invent a God to help them, to give them more women, more money, more children — never a God to help them become more godlike!

"Where the whole world is awake, the sage sleeps. But where the ignorant are asleep, there the sage keeps awake" (Ibid. 69.) — in the world of light where man looks upon himself not as a bird, not as an animal, not as a body, but as infinite spirit, deathless, immortal.

There, where the ignorant are asleep, and do not have time, nor intellect, nor power to understand, there the sage is awake. That is daylight for him.

"As all the rivers of the world constantly pour their waters into the ocean, but the ocean's grand, majestic nature remains undisturbed and unchanged, so even though all the senses bring in sensations from nature, the ocean-like heart of the sage knows no disturbance, knows no fear." (Ibid. 70.)

Let miseries come in millions of rivers and happiness in hundreds! I am no slave to misery! I am no slave to happiness!

Message of the Gita

Now it is for us to see what there is in the Gita.

If we study the Upanishads we notice, in wandering through the mazes of many irrelevant subjects, the sudden introduction of the discussion of a great truth, just as in the midst of a huge wilderness a traveller unexpectedly comes across here and there an exquisitely beautiful rose, with its leaves, thorns, roots, all entangled.

Compared with that, the Gita is like these truths beautifully arranged together in their proper places — like a fine garland or a bouquet of the choicest flowers. The Upanishads deal elaborately with Shraddha in many places, but hardly mention Bhakti. In the Gita, on the other hand, the subject of Bhakti is not only again and again dealt with, but in it, the innate spirit of Bhakti has attained its culmination.

Now let us see some of the main points discussed in the Gita. Wherein lies the originality of the Gita which distinguishes it from all preceding scriptures?

It is this: Though before its advent, Yoga, Jnana, Bhakti, etc. had each its strong adherents, they all quarrelled among themselves, each claiming superiority for his own chosen path; no one ever tried to seek for reconciliation among these different paths.

It was the author of the Gita who for the first time tried to harmonise these. He took the best from what all the sects then existing had to offer and threaded them in the Gita. But even where Krishna failed to show a complete reconciliation (Samanvaya) among these warring sects, it was fully accomplished by Ramakrishna Paramahamsa in this nineteenth century.

The next is, Nishkama Karma, or work without desire or attachment. People nowadays understand what is meant by this in various ways. Some say what is implied by being unattached is to become purposeless. If that were its real meaning, then heartless brutes and the walls would be the best exponents of the performance of Nishkama Karma.

Many others, again, give the example of Janaka, and wish themselves to be equally recognised as past masters in the practice of Nishkama Karma! Janaka (lit. father) did not acquire that distinction by bringing forth children, but these people all want to be Janakas, with the sole qualification of being the fathers of a brood of children!

No! The true Nishkama Karmi (performer of work without desire) is neither to be like a brute, nor to be inert, nor heartless. He is not Tamasika but of pure Sattva. His heart is so full of love and sympathy that he can embrace the whole world with his love. The world at large cannot generally comprehend his all-embracing love and sympathy.

The reconciliation of the different paths of Dharma,

and work without desire or attachment — these are the two special characteristics of the Gita.

Let us now read a little from the second chapter.

"Sanjaya said:

To him who was thus overwhelmed with pity and sorrowing, and whose eyes were dimmed with tears, Madhusudana spoke these words.

The Blessed Lord said:

In such a strait, whence comes upon thee, O Arjuna, this dejection, un-Aryan-like, disgraceful, and contrary to the attainment of heaven? Yield not to unmanliness, O son of Pritha! Ill doth it become thee. Cast off this mean faint-heartedness and arise, O scorcher of thine enemies!"

In the Shlokas beginning with, how poetically, how beautifully, has Arjuna's real position been painted!

Then Shri Krishna advises Arjuna; and in the words etc., why is he goading Arjuna to fight? Because it was not that the disinclination of Arjuna to fight arose out of the overwhelming predominance of pure Sattva Guna; it was all Tamas that brought on this unwillingness.

The nature of a man of Sattva Guna is, that he is equally calm in all situations in life — whether it be prosperity or adversity. But Arjuna was afraid, he was overwhelmed with pity. That he had the instinct and the inclination to fight is proved by the simple fact that he came to the battle-field with no other purpose than that.

Frequently in our lives also such things are seen to happen. Many people think they are Sattvika by nature, but they are really nothing but Tamasika. Many living in an uncleanly way regard themselves as Paramahamsas!

Why? Because the Shastras say that Paramahamsas live like one inert, or mad, or like an unclean spirit. Paramahamsas are compared to children, but here it should be understood that the comparison is one-sided. The Paramahamsa and the child are not one and non-different. They only appear similar, being the two extreme poles, as it were.

One has reached to a state beyond Jnana, and the other has not got even an inkling of Jnana. The quickest and the gentlest vibrations of light are both beyond the reach of our ordinary vision; but in the one it is intense heat, and in the other it may be said to be almost without any heat.

So it is with the opposite qualities of Sattva and Tamas. They seem in some respects to be the same, no doubt, but there is a world of difference between them. The Tamoguna loves very much to array itself in the garb of the Sattva. Here, in Arjuna, the mighty warrior, it has come under the guise of Daya (pity).

In order to remove this delusion which had overtaken Arjuna, what did the Bhagavan say? As I always preach that you should not decry a man by calling him a sinner, but that you should draw his attention to the omnipotent power that is in him, in the same way does the Bhagavan speak to Arjuna. — "It doth not befit thee!"

"Thou art Atman imperishable, beyond all evil. Having forgotten thy real nature, thou hast, by thinking thyself a sinner, as one afflicted with bodily evils and mental grief, thou hast made thyself so — this doth not befit thee!"

So says the Bhagavan: — Yield not to unmanliness, O son of Pritha. There is in the world neither sin nor misery, neither disease nor grief; if there is anything in the world which can be called sin, it is this — 'fear'; know that any work which brings out the latent power in thee is Punya (virtue); and that which makes thy body and mind weak is, verily, sin. Shake off this weakness, this faintheartedness! — Thou art a hero, a Vira; this is unbecoming of thee."

If you, my sons, can proclaim this message to the world — — then all this disease, grief, sin, and sorrow will vanish from off the face of the earth in three days. All these ideas of weakness will be nowhere. Now it is everywhere — this current of the vibration of fear. Reverse the current: bring in the opposite vibration, and behold the magic transformation! Thou art omnipotent — go, go to the mouth of the cannon, fear not.

Hate not the most abject sinner, fool; not to his exterior. Turn thy gaze inward, where resides the Paramatman. Proclaim to the whole world with trumpet voice, "There is no sin in thee, there is no misery in thee; thou art the reservoir of omnipotent power. Arise, awake, and manifest the Divinity within!"

If there is anything in the Gita that I like, it is these two verses, coming out strong as the very gist, the very essence, of Krishna's teaching — "He who sees the Supreme Lord dwelling alike in all beings, the Imperishable in things that perish, he sees indeed. For seeing the Lord as the same, everywhere present, he does not destroy the Self by the Self, and thus he goes to the highest goal."

Religions, Experience and Perception

All our knowledge is based upon experience. What we call inferential knowledge, in which we go from the less to the more general, or from the general to the particular, has experience as its basis. In what are called the exact sciences, people easily find the truth, because it appeals to the particular experiences of every human being.

The scientist does not tell you to believe in anything, but he has certain results which come from his own experiences, and reasoning on them when he asks us to believe in his conclusions, he appeals to some universal experience of humanity. In every exact science there is a basis which is common to all humanity, so that we can at once see the truth or the fallacy of the conclusions drawn therefrom.

Now, the question is: Has religion any such basis or not? I shall have to answer the question both in the affirmative and in the negative.

Religion, as it is generally taught all over the world, is said to be based upon faith and belief. In most cases, it consists only of different sets of theories, and that is the reason why we find all religions quarrelling with one another.

These theories, again, are based upon belief. One man says there is a great Being sitting above the clouds and governing the whole universe, and he asks me to believe that solely on the authority of his assertion.

In the same way, I may have my own ideas, which I am asking others to believe, and if they ask a reason, I cannot give them any.

This is why religion and metaphysical philosophy have a bad name nowadays. Every educated man seems to say, "Oh, these religions are only bundles of theories without any standard to judge them by, each man preaching his own pet ideas."

Nevertheless, there is a basis of universal belief in religion, governing all the different theories and all the varying ideas of different sects in different countries. Going to their basis we find that they also are based upon universal experiences.

In the first place, if you analyse all the various religions of the world, you will find that these are divided into two classes, those with a book and those without a book. Those with a book are the strongest, and have the largest number of followers. Those without books have mostly died out, and the few new ones have very small following. Yet, in all of them we find one consensus of opinion, that the truths they teach are the results of the experiences of particular persons.

The Christian asks you to believe in his religion, to believe in Christ and to believe in him as the incarnation of God, to believe in a God, in a soul, and in a better state of that soul. If I ask him for reason, he says he believes in them. But if you go to the fountain-head of Christianity, you will find that it is based upon experience. Christ said he saw God; the disciples said they felt God; and so forth.

Similarly, in Buddhism, it is Buddha's experience. He experienced certain truths, saw them, came in contact with them, and preached them to the world.

So with the Hindus. In their books the writers, who are called Rishis, or sages, declare they experienced certain truths, and these they preach. Thus it is clear that all the religions of the world have been built upon that one universal and adamantine foundation of all our knowledge — direct experience. The teachers all saw God; they all saw their own souls, they saw their future, they saw their eternity, and what they saw they preached.

Only there is this difference that by most of these religions especially in modern times, a peculiar claim is made, namely, that these experiences are impossible at the present day. They were only possible with a few men, who were the first founders of the religions that subsequently bore their names.

At the present time these experiences have become obsolete, and, therefore, we have now to take religion on belief. This I entirely deny. If there has been one experience in this world in any particular branch of knowledge, it absolutely follows that that experience has been possible millions of times before, and will be repeated eternally. Uniformity is the rigorous law of nature; what once happened can happen always.

The teachers of the science of Yoga, therefore, declare that religion is not only based upon the experience of ancient times, but that no man can be religious until he has the same perceptions himself. Yoga is the science which teaches us how to get these perceptions.

It is not much use to talk about religion until one has felt it. Why is there so much disturbance, so much fighting and quarrelling in the name of God? There has been more bloodshed in the name of God than for any other cause, because people never went to the fountain-head; they were content only to give a mental assent to the customs of their forefathers, and wanted others to do the same.

What right has a man to say he has a soul if he does not feel it, or that there is a God if he does not see Him? If there is a God we must see Him, if there is a soul we must perceive it; otherwise it is better not to believe. It is better to be an outspoken atheist than a hypocrite.

The modern idea, on the one hand, with the "learned" is that religion and metaphysics and all search after a Supreme Being are futile; on the other hand, with the semi-educated, the idea seems to be that these things really have no basis; their only value consists in the fact that they furnish strong motive powers for doing good to the world. If men believe in a God, they may become good, and moral, and so make good citizens.

We cannot blame them for holding such ideas, seeing that all the teaching these men get is simply to believe in an eternal rigmarole of words, without any substance behind them. They are asked to live upon words; can they do it?

If they could, I should not have the least regard for human nature. Man wants truth, wants to experience truth for himself; when he has grasped it, realised it, felt it within his heart of hearts, then alone, declare the Vedas, would all doubts vanish, all darkness be scattered, and all crookedness be made straight.

"Ye children of immortality, even those who live in the highest sphere, the way is found; there is a way out of all this darkness, and that is by perceiving Him who is beyond all darkness; there is no other way."

The science of Raja-Yoga proposes to put before humanity a practical and scientifically worked out method of reaching this truth. In the first place, every science must have its own method of investigation. If you want to become an astronomer and sit down and cry "Astronomy! Astronomy!" it will never come to you.

The same with chemistry. A certain method must be followed. You must go to a laboratory, take different substances, mix them up, compound them, experiment with them, and out of that will come a knowledge of chemistry.

I could preach you thousands of sermons, but they would not make you religious, until you practiced the method. These are the truths of the sages of all countries, of all ages, of men pure and unselfish, who had no motive but to do good to the world.

They all declare that they have found some truth higher than what the senses can bring to us, and they invite verification. They ask us to take up the method and practice honestly, and then, if we do not find this higher truth, we will have the right to say there is no truth in the claim, but before we have done that, we are not rational in denying the truth of their assertions. So we must work faithfully using the prescribed methods, and light will come.

In acquiring knowledge we make use of generalisations, and generalisation is based upon observation. We first observe facts, then generalise, and then draw conclusions or principles. The knowledge of the mind, of the internal nature of man, of thought, can never be had until we have first the power of observing the facts that are going on within.

It is comparatively easy to observe facts in the external world, for many instruments have been invented for the purpose, but in the internal world we have no instrument to help us. Yet we know we must observe in order to have a real science. Without a proper analysis, any science will be hopeless — mere theorising. And that is why all thc psychologists have been quarrelling among themselves since the beginning of time, except those few who found out the means of observation.

The science of Raja-Yoga, in the first place, proposes to give us such a means of observing the internal states. The instrument is the mind itself. The power of attention, when properly guided, and directed towards the internal world, will analyse the mind, and illumine facts for us. The powers of the mind are like rays of light dissipated; when they are concentrated, they illumine.

This is our only means of knowledge. Everyone is using it, both in the external and the internal world; but, for the psychologist, the same minute observation has to be directed to the internal world, which the scientific man directs to the external; and this requires a great deal of practice.

From our childhood upwards we have been taught only to pay attention to things external, but never to things internal; hence most of us have nearly lost the faculty of observing the internal mechanism. To turn the mind as it were, inside, stop it from going outside, and then to concentrate all its powers, and throw them upon the mind itself, in order that it may know its own nature, analyse itself, is very hard work. Yet that is the only way to anything which will be a scientific approach to the subject.

What is the use of such knowledge? In the first place, knowledge itself is the highest reward of knowledge, and secondly, there is also utility in it. It will take away all our misery. When by analysing his own mind, man comes face to face, as it were, with something which is never destroyed, something which is, by its own naturc, eternally pure and perfect, he will no more be miserable, no more unhappy.

All misery comes from fear, from unsatisfied desire. Man will find that he never dies, and then he will have no more fear of death. When he knows that he is perfect, he will have no more vain desires, and both these causes being absent, there will be no more misery — there will be perfect bliss, even while in this body.

There is only one method by which to attain this knowledge, that which is called concentration. The chemist in his laboratory concentrates all the energies of his mind into one focus, and throws them upon the materials he is analysing, and so finds out their secrets. The astronomer concentrates all the energies of his mind and projects them through his telescope upon the skies; and the stars, the sun, and the moon, give up their secrets to him.

The more I can concentrate my thoughts on the matter on which I am talking to you, the more light I can throw upon you. You are listening to me, and the more you concentrate your thoughts, the more clearly you will grasp what I have to say.

How has all the knowledge in the world been gained but by the concentration of the powers of the mind? The world is ready to give up its secrets if we only know how to knock, how to give it the necessary blow. The strength and force of the blow come through concentration. There is no limit to the power of the human mind. The more concentrated it is, the more power is brought to bear on one point; that is the secret.

It is easy to concentrate the mind on external things, the mind naturally goes outwards; but not so in the case of religion, or psychology, or metaphysics, where the subject and the object, are one. The object is internal, the mind itself is the object, and it is necessary to study the mind itself — mind studying mind.

We know that there is the power of the mind called reflection. I am talking to you. At the same time I am standing aside, as it were, a second person, and knowing and hearing what I am talking. You work and think at the same time, while a portion of your mind stands by and sees what you are thinking.

The powers of the mind should be concentrated and turned back upon itself, and as the darkest places reveal their secrets before the penetrating rays of the sun, so will this concentrated mind penetrate its own innermost secrets. Thus will we come to the basis of belief, the real genuine religion. We will perceive for ourselves whether we have souls, whether life is of five minutes or of eternity, whether there is a God in the universe or more. It will all be revealed to us.

This is what Raja-Yoga proposes to teach. The goal of all its teaching is how to concentrate the minds, then, how to discover the innermost recesses of our own minds, then, how to generalise their contents and form our own conclusions from them. It, therefore, never asks the question what our religion is, whether we are Deists or Atheists, whether Christians, Jews, or Buddhists. We are human beings; that is sufficient. Every human being has the right and the power to seek for religion. Every human being has the right to ask the reason, why, and to have his question answered by himself, if he only takes the trouble.

So far, then, we see that in the study of this Raja-Yoga no faith or belief is necessary. Believe nothing until you find it out for yourself; that is what it teaches us. Truth requires no prop to make it stand.

Do you mean to say that the facts of our awakened state require any dreams or imaginings to prove them? Certainly not. This study of Raja-Yoga takes a long time and constant practice. A part of this practice is physical, but in the main it is mental.

As we proceed we shall find how intimately the mind is connected with the body. If we believe that the mind is simply a finer part of the body, and that mind acts upon the body, then it stands to reason that the body must react upon the mind. If the body is sick, the mind becomes sick also. If the body is healthy, the mind remains healthy and strong. When one is angry, the mind becomes disturbed.

Similarly when the mind is disturbed, the body also becomes disturbed. With the majority of mankind the mind is greatly under the control of the body, their mind being very little developed. The vast mass of humanity is very little removed from the animals.

Not only so, but in many instances, the power of control in them is little higher than that of the lower animals. We have very little command of our minds. Therefore to bring that command about, to get that control over body and mind, we must take certain physical helps. When the body is sufficiently controlled, we can attempt the manipulation of the mind. By manipulating the mind, we shall be able to bring it under our control, make it work as we like, and compel it to concentrate its powers as we desire.

According to the Raja-Yogi, the external world is but the gross form of the internal, or subtle. The finer is always the cause, the grosser the effect. So the external world is the effect, the internal the cause. In the same way external forces are simply the grosser parts, of which the internal forces are the finer. The man who has discovered and learned how to manipulate the internal forces will get the whole of nature under his control.

The Yogi proposes to himself no less a task than to master the whole universe, to control the whole of nature. He wants to arrive at the point where what we call "nature's laws" will have no influence over him, where he will be able to get beyond them all. He will be master of the whole of nature, internal and external.

The progress and civilisation of the human race simply mean controlling this nature.

Different races take to different processes of controlling nature. Just as in the same society some individuals want to control the external nature, and others the internal, so, among races, some want to control the external nature, and others the internal. Some say that by controlling internal nature we control everything. Others that by controlling external nature we control everything.

Carried to the extreme both are right, because in nature there is no such division as internal or external. These are fictitious limitations that never existed. The externalists and the internalists are destined to meet at the same point, when both reach the extreme of their knowledge. Just as a physicist, when he pushes his knowledge to its limits, finds it melting away into metaphysics, so a metaphysician will find that what he calls mind and matter are but apparent distinctions, the reality being One.

The end and aim of all science is to find the unity, the One out of which the manifold is being manufactured, that One existing as many. Raja-Yoga proposes to start from the internal world, to study internal nature, and through that, control the whole — both internal and external. It is a very old attempt. India has been its special stronghold, but it was also attempted by other nations.

In Western countries it was regarded as mysticism and people who wanted to practice it were either burned or killed as witches and sorcerers. In India, for various reasons, it fell into the hands of persons who destroyed ninety per cent of the knowledge, and tried to make a great secret of the remainder. In modern times many so-called teachers have arisen in the West worse than those of India, because the latter knew something, while these modern exponents know nothing.

Anything that is secret and mysterious in these systems of Yoga should be at once rejected. The best guide in life is strength. In religion, as in all other matters, discard everything that weakens you, have nothing to do with it. Mystery-mongering weakens the human brain. It has well-nigh destroyed Yoga — one of the grandest of sciences.

From the time it was discovered, more than four thousand years ago, Yoga was perfectly delineated, formulated, and preached in India. It is a striking fact that the more modern the commentator the greater the mistakes he makes, while the more ancient the writer the more rational he is. Most of the modern writers talk of all sorts of mystery.

Thus Yoga fell into the hands of a few persons who made it a secret, instead of letting the full blaze of daylight and reason fall upon it. They did so that they might have the powers to themselves.

In the first place, there is no mystery in what I teach. What little I know I will tell you. So far as I can reason it out I will do so, but as to what I do not know I will simply tell you what the books say. It is wrong to believe blindly. You must exercise your own reason and judgment; you must practice, and see whether these things happen or not.

Just as you would take up any other science, exactly in the same manner you should take up this science for study. There is neither mystery nor danger in it. So far as it is true, it ought to be preached in the public streets, in broad daylight. Any attempt to mystify these things is productive of great danger.

Before proceeding further, I will tell you a little of the Sankhya philosophy, upon which the whole of Raja-Yoga is based.

According to the Sankhya philosophy, the genesis of perception is as follows: the affections of external objects are carried by the outer instruments to their respective brain centres or organs, the organs carry the affections to the mind, the mind to the determinative faculty, from this the Purusha (the soul) receives them, when perception results.

Next he gives the order back, as it were, to the motor centres to do the needful. With the exception of the Purusha all of these are material, but the mind is much finer matter than the external instruments. That material of which the mind is composed goes also to form the subtle matter called the Tanmatras. These become gross and make the external matter.

That is the psychology of the Sankhya. So that between the intellect and the grosser matter outside there is only a difference in degree. The Purusha is the only thing which is immaterial. The mind is an instrument, as it were, in the hands of the soul, through which the soul catches external objects. The mind is constantly changing and vacillating, and can, when perfected, either attach itself to several organs, to one, or to none.

For instance, if I hear the clock with great attention, I will not, perhaps, see anything although my eyes may be open, showing that the mind was not attached to the seeing organ, while it was to the hearing organ. But the perfected mind can be attached to all the organs simultaneously. It has the reflexive power of looking back into its own depths.

This reflexive power is what the Yogi wants to attain; by concentrating the powers of the mind, and turning them inward, he seeks to know what is happening inside. There is in this no question of mere belief; it is the analysis arrived at by certain philosophers.

Modern physiologists tell us that the eyes are not the organ of vision, but that the organ is in one of the nerve centres of the brain, and so with all the senses; they also tell us that these centres are formed of the same material as the brain itself. The Sankhyas also tell us the same thing The former is a statement on the physical side, and the latter on the psychological side; yet both are the same. Our field of research lies beyond this.

The Yogi proposes to attain that fine state of perception in which he can perceive all the different mental states. There must be mental perception of all of them. One can perceive how the sensation is travelling, how the mind is receiving it, how it is going to the determinative faculty, and how this gives it to the Purusha. As each science requires certain preparations and has its own method, which must be followed before it could be understood, even so in Raja-Yoga.

Certain regulations as to food are necessary; we must use that food which brings us the purest mind. If you go into a menagerie, you will find this demonstrated at once. You see the elephants, huge animals, but calm and gentle; and if you go towards the cages of the lions and tigers, you find them restless, showing how much difference has been made by food.

All the forces that are working in this body have been produced out of food; we see that every day. If you begin to fast, first your body will get weak, the physical forces will suffer; then after a few days, the mental forces will suffer also.

First, memory will fail. Then comes a point, when you are not able to think, much less to pursue any course of reasoning. We have, therefore, to take care what sort of food we eat at the beginning, and when we have got strength enough, when our practice is well advanced, we need not be so careful in this respect.

While the plant is growing it must be hedged round, lest it be injured; but when it becomes a tree, the hedges are taken away. It is strong enough to withstand all assaults.

A Yogi must avoid the two extremes of luxury and austerity. He must not fast, nor torture his flesh. He who does so, says the Gita, cannot be a Yogi: He who fasts, he who keeps awake, he who sleeps much, he who works too much, he who does no work, none of these can be a Yogi (Gita, VI, 16).

Knowing God

Let us speak to all the nations of the world in the language of the Vedas: Vain are your fights and your quarrels; have you seen God whom you want to preach? If you have not seen, vain is your preaching; you do not know what you say; and if you have seen God, you will not quarrel, your very face will shine.

An ancient sage of the Upanishads sent his son out to learn about Brahman, and the child came back, and the father asked, "what have you learnt?" The child replied he had learnt so many sciences. But the father said, "That is nothing, go back."

And the son went back, and when he returned again the father asked the same question, and the same answer came from the child. Once more he had to go back.

And the next time he came, his whole face was shining; and his father stood up and declared, "Ay, today, my child, your face shines like a knower of Brahman."

When you have known God, your very face will be changed, your voice will be changed, your whole appearance will he changed. You will be a blessing to mankind; none will be able to resist the Rishi. This is the Rishihood, the ideal in our religion.

The rest, all these talks and reasonings and philosophies and dualisms and monisms, and even the Vedas themselves are but preparations, secondary things. The other is primary. The Vedas, grammar, astronomy, etc., all these are secondary; that is supreme knowledge which makes us realise the Unchangeable One.

Those who realised are the sages whom we find in the Vedas; and we understand how this Rishi is the name of a type, of a class, which every one of us, as true Hindus, is expected to become at some period of our life, and becoming which, to the Hindu, means salvation. Not belief in doctrines, not going to thousands of temples, nor bathing in all the rivers in the world, but becoming the Rishi, the Mantra-drashta — that is freedom, that is salvation.

Coming down to later times, there have been great world-moving sages, great Incarnations of whom there have been many; and according to the Bhagavata, they also are infinite in number, and those that are worshipped most in India are Rama and Krishna.

Rama, the ancient idol of the heroic ages, the embodiment of truth, of morality, the ideal son, the ideal husband, the ideal father, and above all, the ideal king, this Rama has been presented before us by the great sage Valmiki. No language can be purer, none chaster, none more beautiful and at the same time simpler than the language in which the great poet has depicted the life of Rama.

And what to speak of Sita? You may exhaust the

literature of the world that is past, and I may assure you that you will have to exhaust the literature of the world of the future, before finding another Sita. Sita is unique; that character was depicted once and for all. There may have been several Ramas, perhaps, but never more than one Sita!

She is the very type of the true Indian woman, for all the Indian ideals of a perfected woman have grown out of that one life of Sita; and here she stands these thousands of years, commanding the worship of every man, woman, and child throughout the length and breadth of the land of Aryavarta.

There she will always be, this glorious Sita, purer than purity itself, all patience, and all suffering. She who suffered that life of suffering without a murmur, she the ever-chaste and ever-pure wife, she the ideal of the people, the ideal of the gods, the great Sita, our national God she must always remain.

And every one of us knows her too well to require much delineation. All our mythology may vanish, even our Vedas may depart, and our Sanskrit language may vanish for ever, but so long as there will be five Hindus living here, even if only speaking the most vulgar patois, there will be the story of Sita present.

Mark my words: Sita has gone into the very vitals of

our race. She is there in the blood of every Hindu man and woman; we are all children of Sita. Any attempt to modernise our women, if it tries to take our women away from that ideal of Sita, is immediately a failure, as we see every day. The women of India must grow and develop in the footprints of Sita, and that is the only way.

The next is He who is worshipped in various forms, the favourite ideal of men as well as of women, the ideal of children, as well as of grown-up men. I mean He whom the writer of the Bhagavata was not content to call an Incarnation but says, "The other Incarnations were but parts of the Lord. He, Krishna, was the Lord Himself."

And it is not strange that such adjectives are applied to him when we marvel at the many-sidedness of his character. He was the most wonderful Sannyasin, and the most wonderful householder in one; he had the most wonderful amount of Rajas, power, and was at the same time living in the midst of the most wonderful renunciation.

Krishna can never be understood until you have studied the Gita, for he was the embodiment of his own teaching. Every one of these Incarnations came as a living illustration of what they came to preach.

Krishna, the preacher of the Gita, was all his life the

embodiment of that Song Celestial; he was the great illustration of non-attachment. He gives up his throne and never cares for it. He, the leader of India, at whose word kings come down from their thrones, never wants to be a king. He is the simple Krishna, ever the same Krishna who played with the Gopis.

Ah, that most marvellous passage of his life, the most difficult to understand, and which none ought to attempt to understand until he has become perfectly chaste and pure, that most marvellous expansion of love, allegorised and expressed in that beautiful play at Vrindaban, which none can understand but he who has become mad with love, drunk deep of the cup of love! Who can understand the throes of the lore of the Gopis — the very ideal of love, love that wants nothing, love that even does not care for heaven, love that does not care for anything in this world or the world to come?

And here, my friends, through this love of the Gopis has been found the only solution of the conflict between the Personal and the Impersonal God. We know how the Personal God is the highest point of human life; we know that it is philosophical to believe in an Impersonal God immanent in the universe, of whom everything is but a manifestation. At the same time our souls hanker after something concrete, something which we want to grasp, at whose feet we can pour out our soul, and so on.

The Personal God is therefore the highest conception of human nature. Yet reason stands aghast at such an idea. It is the same old, old question which you find discussed in the Brahma-Sutras, which you find Draupadi discussing with Yudhishthira in the forest: If there is a Personal God, all-merciful, all-powerful, why is the hell of an earth here, why did He create this? — He must be a partial God.

There was no solution, and the only solution that can be found is what you read about the love of the Gopis. They hated every adjective that was applied to Krishna; they did not care to know that he was the Lord of creation, they did not care to know that he was almighty, they did not care to know that he was omnipotent, and so forth. The only thing they understood was that he was infinite Love, that was all.

The Gopis understood Krishna only as the Krishna of Vrindaban. He, the leader of the hosts, the King of kings, to them was the shepherd, and the shepherd for ever. "I do not want wealth, nor many people, nor do I want learning; no, not even do I want to go to heaven. Let one be born again and again, but Lord, grant me this, that I may have love for Thee, and that for love's sake."

A great landmark in the history of religion is here, the ideal of love for love's sake, work for work's sake, duty for duty's sake, and it for the first time fell from the lips of the greatest of Incarnations, Krishna, and for the first time in the history of humanity, upon the soil of India. The religions of fear and of temptations were gone for ever, and in spite of the fear of hell and temptation of enjoyment in heaven, came the grandest of ideals, love for love's sake, duty for duty's sake, work for work's sake.

And what a love! I have told you just now that it is very difficult to understand the love of the Gopis. There are not wanting fools, even in the midst of us, who cannot understand the marvellous significance of that most marvellous of all episodes.

There are, let me repeat, impure fools, even born of our blood, who try to shrink from that as if from something impure. To them I have only to say, first make yourselves pure; and you must remember that he who tells the history of the love of the Gopis is none else but Shuka Deva.

The historian who records this marvellous love of the Gopis is one who was born pure, the eternally pure Shuka, the son of Vyasa. So long as there its selfishness in the heart, so long is love of God impossible; it is nothing but shopkeeping: "I give you something; O Lord, you give me something in return"; and says the Lord, "If you do not do this, I will take good care of you when you die. I will roast you all the rest of your lives. perhaps", and so on.

So long as such ideas are in the brain, how can one understand the mad throes of the Gopis' love? "O for one, one kiss of those lips! One who has been kissed by Thee, his thirst for Thee increases for ever, all sorrows vanish, and he forgets love for everything else but for Thee and Thee alone."

Ay, forget first the love for gold, and name and fame, and for this little trumpery world of ours. Then, only then, you will understand the love of the Gopis, too holy to be attempted without giving up everything, too sacred to be understood until the soul has become perfectly pure.

People with ideas of sex, and of money, and of fame, bubbling up every minute in the heart, daring to criticise and understand the love of the Gopis! That is the very essence of the Krishna Incarnation.

Even the Gita, the great philosophy itself, does not compare with that madness, for in the Gita the disciple is taught slowly how to walk towards the goal, but here is the madness of enjoyment, the drunkenness of love, where disciples and teachers and teachings and books and all these things have become one; even the ideas of fear, and God, and heaven — everything has been thrown away. What remains is the madness of love.

It is forgetfulness of everything, and the lover sees nothing in the world except that Krishna and Krishna alone, when the face of every being becomes a Krishna, when his own face looks like Krishna, when his own soul has become tinged with the Krishna colour. That was the great Krishna!

Do not waste your time upon little details. Take up the framework, the essence of the life. There may be many historical discrepancies, there may be interpolations in the life of Krishna. All these things may be true; but, at the same time, there must have been a basis, a foundation for this new and tremendous departure.

Taking the life of any other sage or prophet, we find that that prophet is only the evolution of what had gone before him, we find that that prophet is only preaching the ideas that had been scattered about his own country even in his own times. Great doubts may exist even as to whether that prophet existed or not.

But here, I challenge any one to show whether these things, these ideals — work for work's sake, love for love's sake, duty for duty's sake, were not original ideas with Krishna, and as such, there must have been someone with whom these ideas originated. They could not have been borrowed from anybody else. They were not floating about in the atmosphere when Krishna was born.

But the Lord Krishna was the first preacher of this; his disciple Vyasa took it up and preached it unto mankind. This is the highest idea to picture. The highest thing we can get out of him is Gopijanavallabha, the Beloved of the Gopis of Vrindaban.

When that madness comes in your brain, when you understand the blessed Gopis, then you will understand what love is. When the whole world will vanish, when all other considerations will have died out, when you will become pure-hearted with no other aim, not even the search after truth, then and then alone will come to you the madness of that love, the strength and the power of that infinite love which the Gopis had, that love for love's sake.

That is the goal. When you have got that, you have got everything.

To come down to the lower stratum — Krishna, the preacher of the Gita. Ay, there is an attempt in India now which is like putting the cart before the horse. Many of our people think that Krishna as the lover of the Gopis is something rather uncanny, and the Europeans do not like it much. Dr. So-and-so does not like it.

Certainly then, the Gopis have to go! Without the sanction of Europeans how can Krishna live? He cannot! In the Mahabharata there is no mention of the Gopis except in one or two places, and those not very remarkable places. In the prayer of Draupadi there is mention of a Vrindaban life, and in the speech of Shishupala there is again mention of this Vrindaban.

All these are interpolations! What the Europeans do not want: must be thrown off. They are interpolations, the mention of the Gopis and of Krishna too!

Well, with these men, steeped in commercialism, where even the ideal of religion has become commercial, they are all trying to go to heaven by doing something here; the bania wants compound interest, wants to lay by something here and enjoy it there. Certainly the Gopis have no place in such a system of thought. From that ideal lover we come down to the lower stratum of Krishna, the preacher of the Gita.

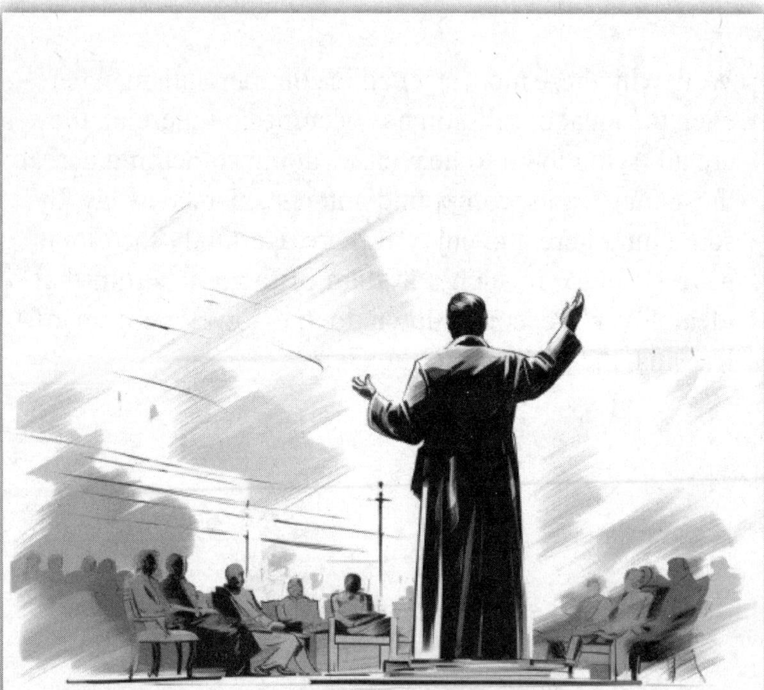

The Gita and the Vedas

Than the Gita no better commentary on the Vedas has been written or can be written. The essence of the Shrutis, or of the Upanishads, is hard to be understood, seeing that there are so many commentators, each one trying to interpret in his own way.

Then the Lord Himself comes, He who is the inspirer of the Shrutis, to show us the meaning of them, as the preacher of the Gita, and today India wants nothing better, the world wants nothing better than that method of interpretation. It is a wonder that subsequent interpreters of the scriptures, even commenting upon the Gita, many times could not catch the meaning, many times could not catch the drift.

For what do you find in the Gita, and what in modern commentators? One non-dualistic commentator takes up an Upanishad; there are so many dualistic passages, and he twists and tortures them into some meaning, and wants to bring them all into a meaning of his own. If a dualistic commentator comes, there are so many nondualistic texts which he begins to torture, to bring them all round to dualistic meaning.

But you find in the Gita there is no attempt at torturing any one of them. They are all right, says the Lord; for slowly and gradually the human soul rises up and up, step after step, from the gross to the fine, from the fine to the finer, until it reaches the Absolute, the goal. That is what is in the Gita.

Even the Karma Kanda is taken up, and it is shown that although it cannot give salvation direct; but only indirectly, yet that is also valid; images are valid indirectly; ceremonies, forms, everything is valid only with one condition, purity of the heart.

For worship is valid and leads to the goal if the heart is pure and the heart is sincere; and all these various modes of worship are necessary, else why should they be there? Religions and sects are not the work of hypocrites and wicked people who invented all these to get a little money, as some of our modern men want to think.

However reasonable that explanation may seem, it is not true, and they were not invented that way at all. They are the outcome of the necessity of the human soul. They are all here to satisfy the hankering and thirst of different classes of human minds, and you need not preach against them. The day when that necessity will cease, they will vanish along with the cessation of that necessity; and so long as that necessity remains, they must be there in spite of your preaching, in spite of your criticism.

You may bring the sword or the gun into play, you may deluge the world with human blood, but so long as there is a necessity for idols, they must remain. These forms, and all the various steps in religion will remain, and we understand from the Lord Shri Krishna why they

Our first duty is not to hate ourselves, because to advance we must have faith in ourselves first and then in God. He who has no faith in himself can never have faith in God. Therefore, the only alternative remaining to us is to recognise that duty and morality vary under different circumstances; not that the man who resists evil is doing what is always and in itself wrong, but that in the different circumstances in which he is placed it may become even his duty to resist evil.

Such is the central idea of Karma-Yoga. The Karma-Yogi is the man who understands that the highest ideal is non-resistance, and who also knows that this non-resistance is the highest manifestation of power in actual possession, and also what is called the resisting of evil is but a step on the way towards the manifestation of this highest power, namely, non-resistance.

Before reaching this highest ideal, man's duty is to resist evil; let him work, let him fight, let him strike straight from the shoulder. Then only, when he has gained the power to resist, will non-resistance be a virtue.

On Krishna

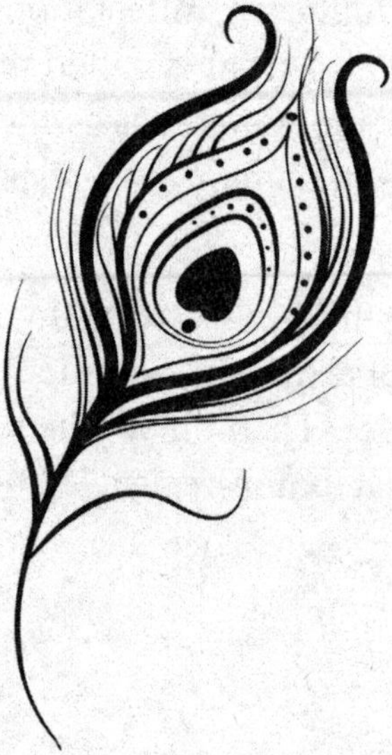

The greatest incident of the war was the marvellous and immortal poem of the Gita, the Song Celestial. It is the popular scripture of India and the loftiest of all teachings. It consists of a dialogue held by Arjuna with Krishna, just before the commencement of the fight on the battle-field of Kurukshetra.

I would advise those of you who have not read that book to read it. If you only knew how much it has influenced your own country even! If you want to know the source of Emerson's inspiration, it is this book, the Gita. He went to see Carlyle, and Carlyle made him a present of the Gita; and that little book is responsible for the Concord Movement. All the broad movements in America, in one way or other, are indebted to the Concord party.

The central figure of the Gita is Krishna. As you worship Jesus of Nazareth as God come down as man so the Hindus worship many Incarnations of God. They believe in not one or two only, but in many, who have come down from time to time, according to the needs of the world, for the preservation of Dharma and destruction of wickedness. Each sect has one, and Krishna is one of them.

Krishna, perhaps, has a larger number of followers in India than any other Incarnation of God. His followers hold that he was the most perfect of those Incarnations. Why? "Because," they say, "look at Buddha and other Incarnations: they were only monks, and they had no sympathy for married people. How could they have? But look at Krishna: he was great as a son, as a king, as a father, and all through his life he practiced the marvellous teachings which he preached."

"He who in the midst of the greatest activity finds the sweetest peace, and in the midst of the greatest calmness is most active, he has known the secret of life."

Krishna shows the way how to do this — by being non-attached: do everything but do not get identified with anything. You are the soul, the pure, the free, all the time; you are the Witness.

Our misery comes, not from work, but by our getting attached to something. Take for instance, money: money is a great thing to have, earn it, says Krishna; struggle hard to get money, but don't get attached to it. So with children, with wife, husband, relatives, fame, everything; you have no need to shun them, only don't get attached.

There is only one attachment and that belongs to the Lord, and to none other. Work for them, love them, do good to them, sacrifice a hundred lives, if need be, for them, but never be attached. His own life was the exact exemplification of that.

Remember that the book which delineates the life of Krishna is several thousand years old, and some parts of his life are very similar to those of Jesus of Nazareth. Krishna was of royal birth; there was a tyrant king, called Kamsa, and there was a prophecy that one would be born of such and such a family, who would be king.

So Kamsa ordered all the male children to be massacred. The father and mother of Krishna were cast by King Kamsa into prison, where the child was born. A light suddenly shone in the prison and the child spoke saying, “I am the Light of the world, born for the good of the world.”

You find Krishna again symbolically represented with cows — “The Great Cowherd,” as he is called. Sages affirmed that God Himself was born, and they went to pay him homage. In other parts of the story, the similarity between the two does not continue.

You who have read the Gita see all through the book that the one idea is non-attachment. Remain unattached.

The heart's love is due to only One. To whom? To Him who never changeth.

Who is that One? It is God. Do not make the mistake of giving the heart to anything that is changing, because that is misery.

You may give it to a man; but if he dies, misery is the result. You may give it to a friend, but he may tomorrow become your enemy. If you give it to your husband, he may one day quarrel with you. You may give it to your wife, and she may die the day after tomorrow.

Now, this is the way the world is going on. So says Krishna in the Gita: The Lord is the only One who never changes. His love never fails. Wherever we are and whatever we do, He is ever and ever the same merciful, the same loving heart.

He never changes, He is never angry, whatever we do. How can God be angry with us? Your babe does many mischievous things: are you angry with that babe? Does not God know what we are going to be? He knows we are all going to be perfect, sooner or later. He has patience, infinite patience.

We must love Him, and everyone that lives — only in and through Him. This is the keynote. You must love the wife, but not for the wife's sake. "Never, O Beloved, is the husband loved on account of the husband, but because the Lord is in the husband."

The Vedanta philosophy says that even in the love of the husband and wife, although the wife is thinking that she is loving the husband, the real attraction is the Lord, who is present there. He is the only attraction, there is no other; but the wife in most cases does not know that it is so, but ignorantly she is doing the right thing, which is, loving the Lord.

Only, when one does it ignorantly, it may bring pain. If one does it knowingly, that is salvation. This is what our scriptures say. Wherever there is love, wherever there is a spark of joy, know that to be a spark of His presence because He is joy, blessedness, and love itself. Without that there cannot be any love.

This is the trend of Krishna's instruction all the time. He has implanted that upon his race, so that when a Hindu does anything, even if he drinks water, he says "If there is virtue in it, let it go to the Lord."

The Buddhist says, if he does any good deed, "Let the merit of the good deed belong to the world; if there is any virtue in what I do, let it go to the world, and let the evils of the world come to me."

The Hindu says he is a great believer in God; the Hindu says that God is omnipotent and that He is the Soul of every soul everywhere; the Hindu says, If I give all my virtues unto Him, that is the greatest sacrifice, and they will go to the whole universe."

Now, this is one phase; and what is the other message of Krishna? "Whosoever lives in the midst of the world, and works, and gives up all the fruit of his action unto the Lord, he is never touched with the evils of the world. Just as the lotus, born under the water, rises up and blossoms above the water, even so is the man who is engaged in the activities of the world, giving up all the fruit of his activities unto the Lord" (Gita, V. 10).

Krishna strikes another note as a teacher of intense activity. Work, work, work day and night, says the Gita. You may ask, "Then, where is peace? If all through life I am to work like a cart-horse and die in harness, what am I here for?"

Krishna says, "Yes, you will find peace. Flying from work is never the way to find peace." Throw off your duties if you can, and go to the top of a mountain; even there the mind is going — whirling, whirling, whirling.

Someone asked a Sannyasin, "Sir, have you found a nice place? How many years have you been travelling in the Himalayas?"

"For forty years," replied the Sannyasin. "There are many beautiful spots to select from, and to settle down in: why did you not do so?"

"Because for these forty years my mind would not allow me to do so."

We all say, “Let us find peace”; but the mind will not allow us to do so.

The Greatness of the Gita

First see the irony of it. Jesus Christ, the God of the Europeans, has taught: Have no enemy, bless them that curse you; whosoever shall smite thee on thy right cheek, turn to him the other also; stop all your work and be ready for the next world; the end of the world is near at hand.

And our Lord in the Gita is saying: Always work with great enthusiasm, destroy your enemies and enjoy the world. But, after all, it turned out to be exactly the reverse of what Christ or Krishna implied.

The Europeans never took the words of Jesus Christ seriously. Always of active habits, being possessed of a tremendous Rajasika nature, they are gathering with great enterprise and youthful ardour the comforts and luxuries of the different countries of the world and enjoying them to their hearts' content. And we are sitting in a corner, with our bag and baggage, pondering on death day and night, and singing,"

नलनीदलगतजलमततिरलं तद्वज्जीवतिमतशियचपलम्—Very tremulous and unsteady is the water on the lotus-leaf; so is the life of man frail and transient"—with the result that it is making our blood run cold and our flesh creep with the fear of Yama, the god of death; and Yama, too, alas, has taken us at our word, as it were—plague and all sorts of maladies have entered into our country!

Who are following the teachings of the Gita? — the Europeans. And who are acting according to the will of

Jesus Christ? — The descendants of Shri Krishna! This must be well understood.

Take the Sermon on the Mount and the Gita — they are simplicity itself. Even the streetwalker can understand them. How grand! In them you find the truth clearly and simply revealed.

The Gita is like a bouquet composed of the beautiful flowers of spiritual truths collected from the Upanishads.

The Gita is the gist of the Vedas. It is not our Bible; the Upanishads are our Bible. It is the gist of the Upanishads and harmonizes the many contradictory parts of the Upanishads.

The Gita is to the Hindus what the New Testament is to the Christians

The greatness of little things, that is what the Gita teaches — bless the old book!

The restless Western atheist or agnostic finds in the Gita or in the Dhammapada the only place where his soul can anchor.

The teachings of Krishna as taught by the Gita are the grandest the world has ever known. He who wrote that wonderful poem was one of those rare souls whose lives sent a wave of regeneration through the world. The human race will never again see such a brain as his who wrote the Gita.

Themes of the Gita: Knowledge

The Vedanta says that the Soul is in its nature Existence absolute, Knowledge absolute, Bliss absolute. But these are not qualities of the Soul: they are one, not three, the essence of the Soul; and it agrees with the Sankhya in thinking that intelligence belongs to nature, inasmuch as it comes through nature.

The Vedanta also shows that what is called intelligence is a compound. For instance, let us examine our perceptions. I see a black-board. How does the knowledge come? What the German philosophers call "the thing-in-itself" of the blackboard is unknown, I can never know it. Let us call it x.

The black-board x acts on my mind, and the mind reacts. The mind is like a lake. Throw a stone in a lake and a reactionary wave comes towards the stone; this wave is not like the stone at all, it is a wave. The black-board x is like a stone which strikes the mind and the mind throws up a wave towards it, and this wave is what we call the black-board.

I see you. You as reality are unknown and unknowable. You are x and you act upon my mind, and the mind throws a wave in the direction from which the impact comes, and that wave is what I call Mr. or Mrs. So-and-so.

There are two elements in the perception, one coming from outside and the other from inside, and the combination of these two, x + mind, is our external universe. All knowledge is by reaction. In the case of a whale it has been determined by calculation how long after its tail is struck, its mind reacts and the whale feels the pain.

Similar is the case with internal perception. The real self within me is also unknown and unknowable. Let us call it y .

When I know myself as so-and-so, it is y + the mind. That y strikes a blow on the mind. So our whole world is x + mind (external), and y + mind (internal), x and y standing for the thing-in-itself behind the external and the internal worlds respectively.

According to Vedanta, the three fundamental factors of consciousness are, I exist, I know, and I am blessed The idea that I have no want, that I am restful, peaceful, that nothing can disturb me, which comes from time to time, is the central fact of our being, the basic principle of our life; and when it becomes limited, and becomes a compound, it manifests itself as existence phenomenal, knowledge phenomenal, and love.

Every man exists, and every man must know, and every man is mad for love. He cannot help loving. Through all existence, from the lowest to the highest, all must love. The y, the internal thing-in-itself, which, combining with mind, manufactures existence, knowledge, and love, is called by the Vedantists. Existence absolute, Knowledge absolute, Bliss absolute. That real existence is limitless, unmixed, uncombined, knows no change, is the free soul; when it gets mixed up, muddled up, as it were, with the mind, it becomes what we call individual existence. It is plant life, animal life, human life, just as universal space is cut off in a room, in a jar, and so on.

And that real knowledge is not what we know, not intuition, nor reason, nor instinct. When that degenerates and is confused, we call it intuition; when it degenerates more, we call it reason; and when it degenerates still more, we call it instinct. That knowledge itself is Vijnana, neither intuition, nor reason nor instinct.

The nearest expression for it is all-knowingness. There is no limit to it, no combination in it. That bliss, when it gets clouded over, we call love, attraction for gross bodies or fine bodies, or for ideas.

This is only a distorted manifestation of that blessedness. Absolute Existence, absolute Knowledge, and absolute Blessedness are not qualities of the soul, but the essence; there is no difference between them and the soul. And the three are one; we see the one thing in three different aspects. They are beyond all relative knowledge.

That eternal knowledge of the Self percolating through

the brain of man becomes his intuition, reason, and so on. Its manifestation varies according to the medium through which it shines. As soul, there is no difference between man and the lowest animal, only the latter's brain is less developed and the manifestation through it which we call instinct is very dull. In a man the brain is much finer, so the manifestation is much clearer, and in the highest man it becomes entirely clear.

So with existence; the existence which we know, the limited sphere of existence, is simply a reflection of that real existence which is the nature of the soul. So with bliss; that which we call love or attraction is but the rejection of the eternal blessedness of the Self. With manifestation comes limitation, but the unmanifested, the essential nature of the soul, is unlimited; to that blessedness there is no limit.

But in love there is limitation. I love you one day, I hate you the next. My love increases one day and decreases the next, because it is only a manifestation.

The first point we will contend with Kapila is his idea of God. Just as the series of modifications of Prakriti, beginning with the individual intellect and ending with the individual body, require a Purusha behind, as the ruler and governor, so, in the Cosmos, the universal intellect, the universal egoism, the universal mind, all universal fine and gross materials, must have a ruler and governor.

How will the cosmic series become complete without the universal Purusha behind them all as the ruler and governor? If you deny a universal Purusha behind the cosmic series, we deny your Purusha behind the individual series.

If it be true that behind the series of graded, evolved individual manifestations, there stands One that is beyond them all, the Purusha who is not composed of matter, the very same logic will apply to the case of universal manifestations. This Universal Self which is beyond the universal modifications of Prakriti is what is called Ishwara, the Supreme Ruler, God.

Now comes the more important point of difference. Can there be more than one Purusha? The Purusha, we have seen, is omnipresent and infinite. The omnipresent, the infinite, cannot be two.

If there are two infinites A and B, the infinite A would limit the infinite B, because the infinite B is not the infinite A, and the infinite A is not the infinite B. Difference in identity means exclusion, and exclusion means limitation. Therefore, A and B, limiting each other, cease to be infinites. Hence, there can be but one infinite, that is, one Purusha.

Now we will take up our x and y and show they are one. We have shown how what we call the external world is x + mind, and the internal world y + mind; x and y are both quantities unknown and unknowable. All difference is due to time, space, and causation.

These are the constituent elements of the mind. No mentality is possible without them. You can never think without time, you can never imagine anything without space, and you can never have anything without causation. These are the forms of the mind. Take them away, and the mind itself does not exist.

All difference is, therefore, due to the mind. According to Vedanta, it is the mind, its forms, that have limited x and y apparently and made them appear as external and internal worlds. But x and y, being both beyond the mind, are without difference and hence one. We cannot attribute any quality to them, because qualities are born of the mind.

That which is qualityless must be one; x is without qualities, it only takes qualities of the mind; so does y; therefore these x and y are one.

The whole universe is one. There is only one Self in the universe, only One Existence, and that One Existence, when it passes through the forms of time, space, and causation, is called by different names, Buddhi, fine matter, gross matter, all mental and physical forms. Everything in the universe is that One, appearing in various forms. When a little part of it comes, as it were, into this network of time, space, and causation, it takes forms; take off the network, and it is all one.

Therefore in the Advaita philosophy, the whole universe is all one in the Self which is called Brahman. That Self when it appears behind the universe is called God. The same Self when it appears behind this little universe, the body, is the soul. This very soul, therefore, is the Self in man. There is only one Purusha, the Brahman of the Vedanta; God and man, analysed, are one in It. The universe is you yourself, the unbroken you; you are throughout the universe.

"In all hands you work, through all mouths you eat, through all nostrils you breathe through all minds you think."

The whole universe is you; the universe is your body; you are the universe both formed and unformed. You are the soul of the universe and its body also. You are God, you are the angels, you are man, you are animals, you are the plants, you are the minerals, you are everything; the manifestation of everything is you. Whatever exists is you. You are the Infinite.

The Infinite cannot be divided. It can have no parts, for each part would be infinite, and then the part would be identical with the whole, which is absurd. Therefore the idea that you are Mr. So-and-so can never be true; it is a day-dream. Know this and be free. This is the Advaita conclusion.

“I am neither the body, nor the organs, nor am I the mind; I am Existence, Knowledge, and Bliss absolute; I am He.”

This is true knowledge; all reason and intellect, and everything else is ignorance. Where is knowledge for me, for I am knowledge itself! Where is life for me, for I am life itself! I am sure I live, for I am life, the One Being, and nothing exists except through me, and in me, and as me. I am manifested through the elements, but I am the free One.

Who seeks freedom? Nobody. If you think that you are bound, you remain bound; you make your own bondage. If you know that you are free, you are free this moment. This is knowledge, knowledge of freedom. Freedom is the goal of all nature.

Themes of the Gita: Love

It is not the place that makes heaven or hell, but the mind. Love knows no fear, there can be no love where it is. In love of any sort external objccts are only suggested by something within — it is one's own ideal projected, and God is the highest ideal that can be conceived of.

Hatred of the world does not drive good men from it, but the world slips away from the great and saintly. The world, the family and social life, are all training grounds, that is all.

When one realizes that God is love, it does not matter what his other attributes are, that is the only essential.

"Bhakti cannot be used to fulfil any desires, itself being the check to all desires." Narada gives these as the signs of love: "When all thoughts, all words, and all deeds are given up unto the Lord, and the least forgetfulness of God makes one intensely miserable, then love has begun."

"This is the highest form of love because therein is no desire for reciprocity, which desire is in all human love."

"A man who has gone beyond social and scriptural usage, he is a Sannyasin. When the whole soul goes to God, when we take refuge only in God, then we know that we are about to get this love."

Obey the scriptures until you are strong enough to do without them; then go beyond them. Books are not an end-all. Verification is the only proof of religious truth.

Each must verify for himself; and no teacher who says, "I have seen, but you cannot", is to be trusted, only that one who says, "You can see too". All scriptures, all truths are Vedas in all times, in all countries; because these truths are to be seen , and any one may discover them.

"When the sun of Love begins to break on the horizon, we want to give up all our actions unto God; and when we forget Him for a moment, it grieves us greatly."

Let nothing stand between God and your love for Him. Love Him, love Him, love Him; and let the world say what it will. Love is of three sorts — one demands, but gives nothing; the second is exchange; and the third is love without thought of return — love like that of the moth for the light.

"Love is higher than work, than Yoga, than knowledge."

Work is merely a schooling for the doer; it can do no good to others. We must work out our own problem;

the prophets only show us how to work. “What you think, you become “, so if you throw your burden on Jesus, you will have to think of Him and thus become like Him — you love Him.

“Extreme love and highest knowledge are one.”

But theorising about God will not do; we must love and work. Give up the world and all worldly things, especially while the “plant” is tender. Day and night think of God and think of nothing else as far as possible. The daily necessary thoughts can all be thought through God. Eat to Him, drink to Him, sleep to Him, see Him in all. Talk of God to others; this is most beneficial.

Get the mercy of God and of His greatest children: these are the two chief ways to God. The company of these children of light is very hard to get; five minutes in their company will change a whole life; and if you really want it enough, one will come to you.

The presence of those who love God makes a place holy, “such is the glory of the children of the Lord”. They are He; and when they speak, their words are scriptures. The place where they have been becomes filled with their vibrations, and those going there feel them and have a tendency to become holy also.

“To such lovers there is no distinction of caste, learning, beauty, birth, wealth, or occupation; because all are His.”

Give up all evil company, especially at the beginning. Avoid worldly company, that will distract your mind. Give up all "me and mine ". To him who has nothing in the universe the Lord comes.

Cut the bondage of all worldly affections; go beyond laziness and all care as to what becomes of you. Never turn back to see the result of what you have done. Give all to the Lord and go on and think not of it.

The whole soul pours in a continuous current to God; there is no time to seek money, or name, or fame, no time to think of anything but God; then will come into our hearts that infinite, wonderful bliss of Love. All desires are but beads of glass.

Love of God increases every moment and is ever new, to be known only by feeling it. Love is the easiest of all, it waits for no logic, it is natural. We need no demonstration, no proof. Reasoning is limiting something by our own minds. We throw a net and catch something, and then say that we have demonstrated it; but never, never can we catch God in a net.

Love should be unrelated. Even when we love wrongly, it is of the true love, of the true bliss; the power is the same, use it as we may. Its very nature is peace and bliss. The murderer when he kisses his baby forgets for an instant all but love.

Give up all self, all egotism, get out of anger, lust, give

all to God. "I am not, but Thou art; the old man is all gone, only Thou remainest." "I am Thou." Blame none; if evil comes, know the Lord is playing with you and be exceeding glad.

Love is beyond time and space, it is absolute.

We must not be extremely attached to anything excepting God. See everything, do everything, but be not attached. As soon as extreme attachment comes, a man loses himself, he is no more master of himself, he is a slave.

If a woman is tremendously attached to a man, she becomes a slave to that man. There is no use in being a slave. There are higher things in this world than becoming a slave to a human being. Love and do good to everybody, but do not become a slave.

In the first place, attachment degenerates us, individually, and in the second place, makes us extremely selfish. Owing to this failing, we want to injure others to do good to those we love. A good many of the wicked deeds done in this world are really done through attachment to certain persons. So all attachment excepting that for good works should be avoided; but love should be given to everybody.

The natural state of this universe is attraction; and that is surely followed by an ultimate disunion. Even so, love is the natural impetus of union in the human heart; and though itself a great cause of misery, properly directed towards the proper object, it brings deliverance. The object of Bhakti is God. Love cannot be without a subject and an object. The object of love again must be at first a being who can reciprocate our love.

Therefore the God of love must be in some sense a human God. He must be a God of love. Aside from the question whether such a God exists or not, it is a fact that to those who have love in their heart this Absolute appears as a God of love, as personal.

The lower forms of worship, which embody the idea of God as a judge or punisher or someone to be obeyed through fear, do not deserve to be called love, although they are forms of worship gradually expanding into higher forms. We pass on to the consideration of love itself.

So long as there is fear, it is not love. Love banishes all fear. A mother with her baby will face a tiger to save her child. The second angle is that love never asks, never begs. The third or the apex is that love loves for the sake of love itself. Even the idea of object vanishes. Love is the only form in which love is loved. This is the highest abstraction and the same as the Absolute.

(Love) can never be the means. The man who says, "I love you for such and such a thing", does not love. Love can never be the means; it must be the perfect end.

What is the end and aim of love? To love God, that is all. Why should one love God? There is no why, because it is not the means. When one can love, that is salvation, that is perfection, that is heaven. What more? What else can be the end? What can you have higher than love?

He who desires God will get Love, unto him God gives Himself. Love is always mutual, reflective. You may hate me, and if I want to love you, you repulse me. But if I persist, in a month or a year you are bound to love me. It is a well-known psychological phenomenon.

As the loving wife thinks of her departed husband, with the same love we must desire the Lord, and then we will find God, and all books and the various sciences would not be able to teach us anything. By reading books we become parrots; no one becomes learned by reading books. If a man reads but one word of love, he indeed becomes learned. So we want first to get that desire.

As soon as a man begins to believe there is a God, he becomes mad with longing to get to Him. Others may go their way, but as soon as a man is sure that there is a much higher life than that which he is leading here, as soon as he feels sure that the senses are not all, that this limited, material body is as nothing compared with the immortal, eternal, undying bliss of the Self, he becomes mad until he finds out this bliss for himself.

And this madness, this thirst, this mania, is what is called the "awakening" to religion, and when that has come, a man is beginning to be religious. But it takes a long time. All these forms and ceremonies, these prayers and pilgrimages, these books, bells, candles, and priests, are the preparations; they take off the impurities from the soul. And when the soul has become pure, it naturally wants to get to the mine of all purity, God Himself.

Just as a piece of iron, which had been covered with the dust of centuries, might be lying near a magnet all the time, and yet not be attracted by it, but as soon as the dust is cleared away, the iron is drawn by the magnet; so, when the human soul, covered with the dust of ages, impurities, wickednesses, and sins, after many births, becomes purified enough by these forms and ceremonies, by doing good to others, loving other beings, its natural spiritual attraction comes, it wakes up and struggles towards God.

Yet, all these forms and symbols are simply the beginning, not true love of God. Love we hear spoken of everywhere Everyone says, "Love God." Men do not know what it into love; if they did, they would not talk so glibly about it. Every man says he can love, and then, in no time, finds out that there is no love in his nature. Every woman says she can love and soon finds out that she cannot.

The world is full of the talk of love, but it is hard to love. Where is love? How do you know that there is love? The first test of love is that it knows no bargaining. So long as you see a man love another only to get something from him, you know that that is not love; it is shopkeeping. Wherever there is any question of buying and selling, it is not love. So, when a man prays to God, "Give me this, and give me that", it is not love. How can it be? I offer you a prayer, and you give me something in return; that is what it is, mere shopkeeping.

A certain great king went to hunt in a forest, and there he happened to meet a sage. He had a little conversation with him and became so pleased with him that he asked him to accept a present from him.

"No," said the sage, "I am perfectly satisfied with my condition; these trees give me enough fruit to eat; these beautiful pure streams supply me with all the water I want; I sleep in these caves. What do I care for your presents, though you be an emperor?"

The emperor said, "Just to purify me, to gratify me, come with me into the city and take some present."

At last the sage consented to go with the emperor, and he was taken into the emperor's palace, where there were gold, jewellery, marble, and most wonderful things. Wealth and power were manifest everywhere.

The emperor asked the sage to wait a minute, while he repeated his prayer, and he went into a corner and began to pray, "Lord, give me more wealth, more children, more territory."

In the meanwhile, the sage got up and began to walk away. The emperor saw him going and went after him. "Stay, Sir, you did not take my present and are going away."

The sage turned to him and said, "Beggar, I do not beg of beggars. What can you give? You have been begging yourself all the time."

That is not the language of love. What is the difference between love and shopkeeping, if you ask God to give you this, and give you that?

The first test of love is that it knows no bargaining. Love is always the giver, and never the taker.

Says the child of God, "If God wants, I give Him my everything, but I do not want anything of Him. I want nothing in this universe. I love Him, because I want to love Him, and I ask no favour in return. Who cares whether God is almighty or not? I do not want any power from Him nor any manifestation of His power. Sufficient for me that He is the God of love. I ask no more question."

The second test is that love knows no fear. So long as man thinks of God as a Being sitting above the clouds, with rewards in one hand and punishments in the other, there can be no love.

Can you frighten one into love? Does the lamb love the lion? The mouse, the cat? The slave, the master? Slaves sometimes simulate love, but is it love? Where do you ever see love in fear? It is always a sham. With love never comes the idea of fear.

Think of a young mother in the street: if a dog barks at her, she flees into the nearest house. The next day she is in the street with her child, and suppose a lion rushes upon the child, where will be her position? Just at the mouth of the lion, protecting her child.

Love conquered all her fear.

So also in the love of God. Who cares whether God is a rewarder or a punisher? That is not the thought of a lover.

Think of a judge when he comes home, what does his wife see in him? Not a judge, or a rewarder or punisher, but her husband, her love. What do his children see in him? Their loving father, not the punisher or rewarder.

So the children of God never see in Him a punisher or a rewarder. It is only people who have never tasted of love that fear and quake. Cast off all fear — though these horrible ideas of God as a punisher or rewarder may have their use in savage minds. Some men, even the most intellectual, are spiritual savages, and these ideas may help them.

But to men who are spiritual, men who are approaching religion, in whom spiritual insight is awakened, such ideas are simply childish, simply foolish. Such men reject all ideas of fear.

The third is a still higher test. Love is always the highest ideal. When one has passed through the first two stages, when one has thrown off all shopkeeping, and cast off all fear, one then begins to realise that love is always the highest ideal.

How many times in this world we see a beautiful woman loving an ugly man? How many times we see a handsome man loving an ugly woman! What is the attraction? Lookers-on only see the ugly man or the ugly woman, but not so the lover; to the lover the beloved is the most beautiful being that ever existed.

How is it? The woman who loves the ugly man takes, as it were, the ideal of beauty which is in her own mind, and projects it on this ugly man; and what she worships and loves is not the ugly man, but her own ideal. That man is, as it were, only the suggestion, and upon that suggestion she throws her own ideal, and covers it; and it becomes her object of worship.

Now, this applies in every case where we love. Many of us have very ordinary looking brothers or sisters; yet the very idea of their being brothers or sisters makes them beautiful to us.

No one in this world can really love anything but God. Man finds out that human love is all hollow. Men cannot love though they talk of it.

The wife says she loves her husband and kisses him; but as soon as he dies, the first thing she thinks about is the bank account, and what she shall do the next day. The husband loves the wife; but when she becomes sick and loses her beauty, or becomes haggard, or makes a mistake, he ceases to care for her. All the love of the world is hypocrisy and hollowness.

A finite subject cannot love, nor a finite object be loved.

When the object of the love of a man is dying every moment, and his mind also is constantly changing as he grows, what eternal love can you expect to find in the world? There cannot be any real love but in God: why then all these loves? These are mere stages. There is a power behind impelling us forward, we do not know where to seek for the real object, but this love is sending us forward in search of it.

Again and again we find out our mistake. We grasp something, and find it slips through our fingers, and then we grasp something else. Thus on and on we go, till at last comes light; we come to God, the only One who loves. His love knows no change and is ever ready to take us in. How long would any of you bear with me if I injured you? He in whose mind is no anger, hatred, or envy, who never loses his balance, dies, or is born, who is he but God?

All the different kinds of love which we see in the world, and with which we are more or less playing merely, have God as the one goal; but unfortunately, man does not know the infinite ocean into which this mighty river of love is constantly flowing, and so, foolishly, he often tries to direct it to little dolls of human beings. The tremendous love for the child that is in human nature is not for the little doll of a child; if you bestow it blindly and exclusively on the child, you will suffer in consequence.

But through such suffering will come the awakening by which you are sure to find out that the love which is in you, if it is given to any human being, will sooner or later bring pain and sorrow as the result. Our love must, therefore, be given to the Highest One who never dies and never changes, to Him in the ocean of whose love there is neither ebb nor flow.

Love must get to its right destination; it must go unto Him who is really the infinite ocean of love. All rivers flow into the ocean. Even the drop of water coming down from the mountain side cannot stop its course after reaching a brook or a river, however big it may be; at last even that drop somehow does find its way to the ocean.

God is the one goal of all our passions and emotions. If you want to be angry, be angry with Him. Chide your Beloved, chide your Friend.

Whom else can you safely chide? Mortal man will not patiently put up with your anger; there will be a reaction. If you are angry with me, I am sure quickly to react, because I cannot patiently put up with your anger.

Say unto the Beloved, "Why do You not come to me; why do You leave me thus alone?"

Where is there any enjoyment but in Him? What enjoyment can there be in little clods of earth? It is the crystallised essence of infinite enjoyment that we have to seek, and that is in God.

Let all our passions and emotions go up unto Him. They are meant for Him, for if they miss their mark and go lower, they become vile; and when they go straight to the mark, to the Lord, even the lowest of them becomes transfigured. All the energies of the human body and mind, howsoever they may express themselves, have the Lord as their one goal, as their Ekayana.

All loves and all passions of the human heart must go to God. He is the Beloved. Whom else can this heart love? He is the most beautiful, the most sublime, He is beauty itself, sublimity itself. Who in this universe is more beautiful than He? Who in this universe is more fit to become the husband than He? Who in this universe is fitter to be loved than He? So let Him be the husband, let Him be the Beloved.

The world presents to us manifold stages of love. We have first to clear the ground. Upon our view of life the whole theory of love will rest.

To think that this world is the aim and end of life is brutal and degenerating. Any man who starts in life with that idea degenerates himself. He will never rise higher, he will never catch this glimpse from behind, he will always be a slave to the senses. He will struggle for the dollar that will get him a few cakes to eat.

Better die than live that life. Slaves of this world, slaves of the senses, let us rouse ourselves; there is something higher than this sense-life.

Do you think that man, the Infinite Spirit was born to be a slave to his eyes, his nose, and his ears? There is an Infinite, Omniscient Spirit behind that can do everything, break every bond; and that Spirit we are, and we get that power through love. This is the ideal we must remember.

The tree receives support and shelter from the hedge that surrounds it when young; but unless the hedge is removed, the growth and strength of that tree will be hindered. Formal worship, as we have seen, is a necessary stage, but gradually by slow growth we outgrow it and come to a higher platform.

When love to God becomes perfect, we think no more of the qualities of God — that He is omnipotent, omnipresent, and all those big adjectives. We do not want anything of God, so we do not care to notice these qualities. Just all we want is love of God. But anthropomorphism still follows us. We cannot get away from our humanity, we cannot jump out of our bodies; so we must love God as we love one another.

There are five steps in human love.

1. The lowest, most commonplace, “peaceful” love, when we look up to our Father for all we want — protection, food, etc.

2. The love which makes us want to serve. Man wants to serve God as his master, the longing to serve dominating every other feeling; and we are indifferent whether the master is good or bad, kind or unkind.

3. The love of a friend, the love of equals — companions, playmates. Man feels God to be his companion.

4. Motherly love. God is looked upon as a child. In India this is considered a higher love than the foregoing, because it has absolutely no element of fear.

5. The love of husband and wife; love for love’s sake — God the perfect, beloved one.

It has been beautifully expressed: “Four eyes meet, a change begins to come into two souls; love comes in the middle between these two souls and makes them one.”

When a man has this last and most perfect form of love, then all desires vanish, forms and doctrines and churches drop away, even the desire for freedom (the end and aim of all religions is freedom from birth and death and other things) is given up. The highest love is the love that is sexless, for it is perfect unity that is expressed in the highest love, and sex differentiates bodies.

It is therefore only in spirit that union is possible. The less we have of the physical idea, the more perfect will be our love; at last all physical thought will be forgotten, and the two souls will become one. We love, love always. Love comes and penetrates through the forms and sees beyond.

It has been said, "The lover sees Helen's beauty in an Ethiopian's brow." The Ethiopian is the suggestion and upon that suggestion the man throws his love.

As the oyster throws over the irritants, it finds in its shell, the substance that turns the irritants into beautiful pearls, so man throws out love, and it is always man's highest ideal that he loves, and the highest ideal is always selfless; so man loves love.

God is love, and we love God — or love love. We only see love, love cannot be expressed. "A dumb man eating butter" cannot tell you what butter is like. Butter is butter, and its qualities cannot be expressed to those who have not tasted it. Love for love's sake cannot be expressed to those who have not felt it.

Love may be symbolised by a triangle. The first angle is, love never begs, never asks for anything; the second, love knows no fear; the third and the apex, love for love's sake.

Through the power of love the senses become finer and higher. The perfect love is very rare in human relation, for human love is almost always interdcpendent and mutual. But God's love is a constant stream, nothing can hurt or disturb it.

When man loves God as his highest ideal, as no beggar, wanting nothing, then is love carried to the extreme of evolution, and it becomes a great power in the universe. It takes a long time to get to these things, and we have to begin by that which is nearest to our nature; some are born to service, some to be mothers in love. Anyhow, the result is with God. We must take advantage of nature.

Bhakti-Yoga: teaches how to love, without any ulterior motives, loving God and loving the good because it is good to do so, not for going to heaven, nor to get children, wealth, or anything else. It teaches them that love itself is the highest recompense of love --- that God Himself is love.

It teaches them to pay all kinds of tribute to God as the Creator, the Omnipresent, Omniscient, Almighty Ruler, the Father and the Mother. The highest phrase that can express Him, the highest idea that the human mind can conceive of Him, is that He is the God of Love. Wherever there is love, it is He.

"Wherever there is any love, it is He, the Lord is present there."

Where the husband kisses the wife, He is there in the kiss; where the mother kisses the child, He is there in the kiss; where friends clasp hands, He, the Lord, is present as the God of Love. When a great man loves and wishes to help mankind, He is there giving freely His bounty out of His love to mankind.

Wherever the heart expands, He is there manifested. This is what the Bhakti-Yoga teaches.

Thus sang the royal Hebrew sage, thus sang they of India. "O beloved, one kiss of Thy lips! Kissed by Thee, one's thirst for Thee increaseth for ever! All sorrows cease, one forgets the past, present, and future, and only thinks of Thee alone." That is the madness of the lover, when all desires have vanished.

"Who cares for salvation? Who cares to be saved? Who cares to be perfect even? Who cares for freedom?" — says the lover. "I do not want wealth, nor even health; I do not want beauty, I do not want intellect: let me be born again and again, amid all the evils that are in the world; I will not complain, but let me love Thee, and that for love's sake."

That is the madness of love which finds expression in these songs. The highest, most expressive, strongest, and most attractive human love is that between man and woman, and, therefore, that language was used in expressing the deepest devotion. The madness of this human love was the faintest echo of the mad love of the saints.

The true lovers of God want to become mad, inebriated with the love of God, to become "God-intoxicated men". They want to drink of the cup of love which has been prepared by the saints and sages of every religion, who have poured their heart's blood into it, and in which hare been concentrated all the hopes of those who have loved God without seeking reward, who wanted love for itself only.

The reward of love is love, and what a reward it is! It is the only thing that takes off all sorrows, the only cup, by the drinking of which this disease of the world vanishes Man becomes divinely mad and forgets that be is man.

Whatever occurs in our life, whether good or bad, is bringing us to Him. One man kills another because of some selfish purpose. But the motive behind is love, whether for himself or for any one else. Whether we do good or evil, the propeller is love. When a tiger kills a buffalo, it is because he or his cubs are hungry.

God is love personified. He is apparent in everything. Everybody is being drawn to Him whether he knows it or not. When a woman loves her husband, she does not understand that it is the divine in her husband that is the great attractive power.

The God of Love is the one thing to be worshipped. So long as we think of Him only as the Creator and Preserver, we can offer Him external worship, but when we get beyond all that and think Him to be Love Incarnate, seeing Him in all things and all things in Him, it is then that supreme Bhakti is attained.

Though the love of a mother is in some ways greater, yet the whole world takes the love of man and woman as the type (of the soul's relation to God). No other has such tremendous idealising power. The beloved actually becomes what he is imagined to be. This love transforms its object.

A great saint said, using the language of a girl, describing love: "Four eyes met. There were changes in two souls. And now I cannot tell whether he is a man and I am a woman, or he is a woman and I a man. This only I remember, two souls were. Love came, and there was one."

In the highest love, union is only of the spirit. All love of any other kind is quickly evanescent. Only the spiritual lasts, and this grows.

Love sees the Ideal. This is the third angle of the triangle. God has been Cause, Creator, Father. Love is the culmination. The mother regrets that her child is humpbacked, but when she has nursed him for a few days, she loves him and thinks him most beautiful.

The lover sees the beauty of Helen in the brow of Ethiopia.

We do not commonly realise what happens. The brow of Ethiopia is merely a suggestion: the man sees Helen. His ideal is thrown upon the suggestion and covers it, as the oyster makes sand into a pearl. God is this ideal, through which man may see all.

Hence we come to love love itself. This love cannot be expressed. No words can utter it. We are dumb about it.

The senses become very much heightened in love. Human love, we must remember, is mixed up with attributes. It is dependent, too, on the other's attitude. Indian languages have words to describe this interdependence of love. The lowest love is selfish; it consists in pleasure of being loved.

We say in India, "One gives the cheek, the other kisses." Above this is mutual love. But this also ceases mutually. True love is all giving. We do not even want to see the other, or to do anything to express our feeling. It is enough to give. It is almost impossible to love a human being like this, but it is possible to love God.

Themes of the Gita: Duty

The ordinary idea of duty everywhere is that every good man follows the dictates of his conscience. But what is it that makes an act a duty?

If a Christian finds a piece of beef before him and does not eat it to save his own life, or will not give it to save the life of another man, he is sure to feel that he has not done his duty. But if a Hindu dares to eat that piece of beef or to give it to another Hindu, he is equally sure to feel that he too has not done his duty; the Hindu's training and education make him feel that way.

In the last century there were notorious bands of robbers in India called thugs; they thought it their duty to kill any man they could and take away his money; the larger the number of men they killed, the better they thought they were.

Ordinarily if a man goes out into the street and shoots down another man, he is apt to feel sorry for it, thinking that he has done wrong. But if the very same man, as a soldier in his regiment, kills not one but twenty, he is certain to feel glad and think that he has done his duty remarkably well.

Therefore we see that it is not the thing done that defines a duty. To give an objective definition of duty is thus entirely impossible.

Yet there is duty from the subjective side. Any action that makes us go Godward is a good action, and is our duty; any action that makes us go downward is evil, and is not our duty.

From the subjective standpoint we may see that certain acts have a tendency to exalt and ennoble us, while certain other acts have a tendency to degrade and to brutalise us. But it is not possible to make out with certainty which acts have which kind of tendency in relation to all persons, of all sorts and conditions.

There is, however, only one idea of duty which has been universally accepted by all mankind, of all ages and sects and countries, and that has been summed up in a Sanskrit aphorism thus: "Do not injure any being; not injuring any being is virtue, injuring any being is sin."

The idea of duty varies much among different nations. In one country, if a man does not do certain things, people will say he has acted wrongly; while if he does those very things in another country, people will say that he did not act rightly — and yet we know that there must be some universal idea of duty. In the same way, one class of society thinks that certain things are among its duty, while another class thinks quite the opposite and would be horrified if it had to do those things.

Two ways are left open to us — the way of the ignorant,

who think that there is only one way to truth and that all the rest are wrong, and the way of the wise, who admit that, according to our mental constitution or the different planes of existence in which we are, duty and morality may vary.

The important thing is to know that there are gradations of duty and of morality — that the duty of one state of life, in one set of circumstances, will not and cannot be that of another.

The Bhagavad-Gita frequently alludes to duties dependent upon birth and position in life. Birth and position in life and in society largely determine the mental and moral attitude of individuals towards the various activities of life. It is therefore our duty to do that work which will exalt and ennoble us in accordance with the ideals and activities of the society in which we are born.

But it must be particularly remembered that the same ideals and activities do not prevail in all societies and countries. Our ignorance of this is the main cause of much of the hatred of one nation towards another.

An American thinks that whatever an American does in accordance with the custom of his country is the best thing to do, and that whoever does not follow his custom must be a very wicked man. A Hindu thinks that his customs are the only right ones and are the best in the world, and that whosoever does not obey them must be the most wicked man living.

This is quite a natural mistake which all of us are apt to make. But it is very harmful; it is the cause of half the uncharitableness found in the world.

When I came to this country and was going through the Chicago Fair, a man from behind pulled at my turban. I looked back and saw that he was a very gentlemanly-looking man, neatly dressed. I spoke to him; and when he found that I knew English, he became very much abashed.

On another occasion in the same Fair another man gave me a push. When I asked him the reason, he also was ashamed and stammered out an apology saying, "Why do you dress that way?"

The sympathies of these men were limited within the range of their own language and their own fashion of dress. Much of the oppression of powerful nations on weaker ones is caused by this prejudice. It dries up their fellow feeling for fellow men.

That very man who asked me why I did not dress as he did and wanted to ill-treat me because of my dress may have been a very good man, a good father, and a good citizen; but the kindliness of his nature died out as soon as he saw a man in a different dress. Strangers are exploited in all countries, because they do not know how to defend themselves; thus they carry home false impressions of the peoples they have seen.

Sailors, soldiers, and traders behave in foreign lands in very queer ways, although they would not dream of doing so in their own country; perhaps this is why the Chinese call Europeans and Americans "foreign devils". They could not have done this if they had met the good, the kindly sides of Western life.

We should always try to see the duty of others through their own eyes, and never judge the customs of other peoples by our own standard. I am not the standard of the universe. I have to accommodate myself to the world, and not the world to me. So we see that environments change the nature of our duties, and doing the duty which is ours at any particular time is the best thing we can do in this world. Let us do that duty which is ours by birth; and when we have done that, let us do the duty which is ours by our position in life and in society.

There is, however, one great danger in human nature, viz that man never examines himself. He thinks he is quite as fit to be on the throne as the king. Even if he is, he must first show that he has done the duty of his own position; and then higher duties will come to him. When we begin to work earnestly in the world, nature gives us blows right and left and soon enables us to find out our position.

No man can long occupy satisfactorily a position for which he is not fit. There is no use in grumbling against nature's adjustment. He who does the lower work is not therefore a lower man. No man is to be judged by the mere nature of his duties, but all should be judged by the manner and the spirit in which they perform them.

Later on we shall find that even this idea of duty undergoes change, and that the greatest work is done only when there is no selfish motive to prompt it. Yet it is work through the sense of duty that leads us to work without any idea of duty; when work will become worship — nay, something higher — then will work be done for its own sake.

We shall find that the philosophy of duty, whether it be in the form of ethics or of love, is the same as in every other Yoga — the object being the attenuating of the lower self, so that the real higher Self may shine forth — the lessening of the frittering away of energies on the lower plane of existence, so that the soul may manifest itself on the higher ones. This is accomplished by the continuous denial of low desires, which duty rigorously requires.

The whole organisation of society has thus been developed, consciously or unconsciously, in the realms of action and experience, where, by limiting selfishness, we open the way to an unlimited expansion of the real nature of man.

Each duty has its own place, and according to the circumstances in which we are placed, we must perform our duties. what is duty for one is not duty for another. At the same time, we do not say that this duty is lowering and the other elevating.

Isolation of the soul from all objects, mental and physical, is the goal; when that is attained, the soul will find that it was alone all the time, and it required no one to make it happy. As long as we require someone else to make us happy, we are slaves. When the Purusha finds that It is free, and does not require anything to complete Itself, that this nature is quite unnecessary, then freedom (Kaivalya) is attained.

Men run after a few dollars and do not think anything of cheating a fellow-being to get those dollars; but if they would restrain themselves, in a few years they would develop such characters as would bring them millions of dollars — if they wanted them. Then their will would govern the universe. But we are all such fools!

What is the use of talking of one's mistakes to the world? They cannot thereby be undone. For what one has done one must suffer; one must try and do better. The world sympathises only with the strong and the powerful.

It is only work that is done as a free-will offering to humanity and to nature that does not bring with it any binding attachment.

Duty of any kind is not to be slighted. A man who does the lower work is not, for that reason only, a lower man than he who does the higher work; a man should not be judged by the nature of his duties, but by the manner in which he does them. His manner of doing them and his power to do them are indeed the test of a man. A shoemaker who can turn out a strong, nice pair of shoes in the shortest possible time is a better man, according to his profession and his work, than a professor who talks nonsense every day of his life.

Every duty is holy, and devotion to duty is the highest form of the worship of God; it is certainly a source of great help in enlightening and emancipating the deluded and ignorance-encumbered souls of the Baddhas — the bound ones.

By doing well the duty which is nearest to us, the duty which is in our hands now, we make ourselves stronger and improving our strength in this manner step by step, we may even reach a state in which it shall be our privilege to do the most coveted and honoured duties in life and in society.

Our first duty is not to hate ourselves, because to advance we must have faith in ourselves first and then in God. He who has no faith in himself can never have faith in God. Therefore, the only alternative remaining to us is to recognise that duty and morality vary under different circumstances; not that the man who resists evil is doing what is always and in itself wrong, but that in the different circumstances in which he is placed it may become even his duty to resist evil.

All great teachers have taught, "Resist not evil," that non-resistance is the highest moral ideal. We all know that, if a certain number of us attempted to put that maxim fully into practice, the whole social fabric would fall to pieces, the wicked would take possession of our properties and our lives, and would do whatever they liked with us. Even if only one day of such non-resistance were practiced, it would lead to disaster.

Yet, intuitively, in our heart of hearts we feel the truth of the teaching "Resist not evil." This seems to us to be the highest ideal; yet to teach this doctrine only would be equivalent to condemning a vast portion of mankind.

Not only so, it would be making men feel that they were always doing wrong, and cause in them scruples of conscience in all their actions; it would weaken them, and that constant self-disapproval would breed more vice than any other weakness would. To the man who has begun to hate himself the gate to degeneration has already opened; and the same is true of a nation.

He who has no faith in himself can never have faith in God. Therefore, the only alternative remaining to us is to recognise that duty and morality vary under different circumstances; not that the man who resists evil is doing what is always and in itself wrong, but that in the different circumstances in which he is placed it may become even his duty to resist evil.

You should cultivate a noble nature by doing your duty. By doing our duty we get rid of the idea of duty; and then and then only we feel everything as done by God. We are but machines in His hand. This body is opaque, God is the lamp. Whatever is going out of the body is God's.

You do not feel it. You feel "I". This is delusion. You must learn calm submission to the will of God. Duty is the best school for it. This duty is morality.

Drill yourself to be thoroughly submissive. Get rid of the "I". No humbuggism. Then you can get rid of the idea of duty; for all is His. Then you go on naturally, forgiving, forgetting, etc.

Our religion always presents different gradations of

duty and religion to different people.

Duty is seldom sweet. It is only when love greases its wheels that it runs smoothly; it is a continuous friction otherwise.

How else could parents do their duties to their children, husbands to their wives, and vice versa? Do we not meet with cases of friction every day in our lives? Duty is sweet only through love, and love shines in freedom alone.

Yet is it freedom to be a slave to the senses, to anger, to jealousies and a hundred other petty things that must occur every day in human life? In all these little roughnesses that we meet with in life, the highest expression of freedom is to forbear.

Women, slaves to their own irritable, jealous tempers, are apt to blame their husbands, and assert their own "freedom", as they think, not knowing that thereby they only prove that they are slaves. So it is with husbands who eternally find fault with their wives.

There is a sage in India, a great Yogi, one of the most wonderful men I have ever seen in my life. He is a peculiar man, he will not teach any one; if you ask him a question he will not answer. It is too much for him to take up the position of a teacher, he will not do it. If you ask a question, and wait for some days, in the course of conversation he will bring up the subject, and wonderful light will he throw on it.

He told me once the secret of work, "Let the end and the means be joined into one." When you are doing any work, do not think of anything beyond. Do it as worship, as the highest worship, and devote your whole life to it for the time being.

Thus, in the story, the Vyadha and the woman did their duty with cheerfulness and whole-heartedness; and the result was that they became illuminated, clearly showing that the right performance of the duties of any station in life, without attachment to results, leads us to the highest realisation of the perfection of the soul.

It is the worker who is attached to results that grumbles about the nature of the duty which has fallen to his lot. To the unattached worker all duties are equally good, and form efficient instruments with which selfishness and sensuality may be killed, and the freedom of the soul secured.

We are all apt to think too highly of ourselves. Our duties are determined by our desires to a much larger extent than we are willing to grant. Competition rouses envy, and it kills the kindliness of the heart. To the grumbler all duties are distasteful; nothing will ever satisfy him, and his whole life is doomed to prove a failure.

Let us work on, doing as we go whatever happens to be our duty, and being ever ready to put our shoulders to the wheel. Then surely shall we see the Light!

Karma-Yoga teaches us that the ordinary idea of duty is on the lower plane; nevertheless, all of us have to do our duty. Yet we may see that this peculiar sense of duty is very often a great cause of misery.

Duty becomes a disease with us; it drags us ever forward. It catches hold of us and makes our whole life miserable. It is the bane of human life. This duty, this idea of duty is the midday summer sun which scorches the innermost soul of mankind.

Look at those poor slaves to duty! Duty leaves them no time to say prayers, no time to bathe. Duty is ever on them. They go out and work. Duty is on them!

They come home and think of the work for the next day. Duty is on them! It is living a slave's life, at last dropping down in the street and dying in harness, like a horse.

This is duty as it is understood.

What is duty after all? It is really the impulsion of the flesh, of our attachment; and when an attachment has become established, we call it duty.

It is, so to say, a sort of chronic disease. When it is acute, we call it disease; when it is chronic, we call it nature. It is a disease.

So when attachment becomes chronic, we baptise it with the high sounding name of duty. We strew flowers upon it, trumpets sound for it, sacred texts are said over it, and then the whole world fights, and men earnestly rob each other for this duty's sake.

Duty is good to the extent that it checks brutality. To the lowest kinds of men, who cannot have any other ideal, it is of some good; but those who want to be Karma-Yogis must throw this idea of duty overboard. There is no duty for you and me. Whatever you have to give to the world, do give by all means, but not as a duty. Do not take any thought of that. Be not compelled.

Unity in variety is the plan of creation. However men and women may vary individually, there is unity in the background. The different individual characters and classes of men and women are natural variations in creation.

Hence, we ought not to judge them by the same standard or put the same ideal before them. Such a course creates only an unnatural struggle, and the result is that man begins to hate himself and is hindered from becoming religious and good. Our duty is to encourage every one in his struggle to live up to his own highest ideal, and strive at the same time to make the ideal as near as possible to the truth.

In the material physical world, expansion is life, and contraction is death. Whatever ceases to expand ceases to live. Translating this in the moral world we have: If one would expand, he must love, and when he ceases to love he dies. It is your nature; you must, because that is the only law of life.

Therefore, we must love God for love's sake, so we must do our duty for duty's sake; we must work for work's sake without looking for any reward — know that you are purer and more perfect, know that this is the real temple of God.

Every man should take up his own ideal and endeavour to accomplish it. That is a surer way of progress than taking up other men's ideals, which he can never hope to accomplish.

For instance, we take a child and at once give him the task of walking twenty miles. Either the little one dies, or one in a thousand crawls the twenty miles, to reach the end exhausted and half-dead.

That is like what we generally try to do with the world. All the men and women, in any society, are not of the same mind, capacity, or of the same power to do things; they must have different ideals, and we have no right to sneer at any ideal. Let everyone do the best he can for realising his own ideal.

Nor is it right that I should be judged by your standard or you by mine. The apple tree should not be judged by the standard of the oak, nor the oak by that of the apple. To judge the apple tree you must take the apple standard, and for the oak, its own standard.

Themes of the Gita: Karma

We read in the Bhagavad-Gita again and again that we must all work incessantly. All work is by nature composed of good and evil. We cannot do any work which will not do some good somewhere; there cannot be any work which will not cause some harm somewhere. Every work must necessarily be a mixture of good and evil; yet we are commanded to work incessantly.

Good and evil will both have their results, will produce their Karma. Good action will entail upon us good effect; bad action, bad. But good and bad are both bondages of the soul.

The solution reached in the Gita in regard to this bondage-producing nature of work is that, if we do not attach ourselves to the work we do, it will not have any binding effect on our soul. We shall try to understand what is meant by this "non-attachment to" to work.

This is the one central idea in the Gita: work incessantly, but be not attached to it. Samskara can be translated very nearly by "inherent tendency". Using the simile of a lake for the mind, every ripple, every wave that rises in the mind, when it subsides, does not die out entirely, but leaves a mark and a future possibility of that wave coming out again.

This mark, with the possibility of the wave reappearing, is what is called Samskara. Every work that we do, every movement of the body, every thought that we think, leaves such an impression on the mind-stuff, and even when such impressions are not obvious on the surface, they are sufficiently strong to work beneath the surface, subconsciously.

What we are every moment is determined by the sum total of these impressions on the mind. What I am just at this moment is the effect of the sum total of all the impressions of my past life.

This is really what is meant by character; each man's character is determined by the sum total of these impressions. If good impressions prevail, the character becomes good; if bad, it becomes bad. If a man continuously hears bad words, thinks bad thoughts, does bad actions, his mind will be full of bad impressions; and they will influence his thought and work without his being conscious of the fact.

In fact, these bad impressions are always working, and their resultant must be evil, and that man will be a bad man; he cannot help it. The sum total of these impressions in him will create the strong motive power for doing bad actions. He will be like a machine in the hands of his impressions, and they will force him to do evil. Similarly, if a man thinks good thoughts and does good works, the sum total of these impressions will be good; and they, in a similar manner, will force him to do good even in spite of himself.

When a man has done so much good work and thought

so many good thoughts that there is an irresistible tendency in him to do good in spite of himself and even if he wishes to do evil, his mind, as the sum total of his tendencies, will not allow him to do so; the tendencies will turn him back; he is completely under the influence of the good tendencies. When such is the case, a man's good character is said to be established.

As the tortoise tucks its feet and head inside the shell, and you may kill it and break it in pieces, and yet it will not come out, even so the character of that man who has control over his motives and organs is unchangeably established. He controls his own inner forces, and nothing can draw them out against his will.

By this continuous reflex of good thoughts, good impressions moving over the surface of the mind, the tendency for doing good becomes strong, and as the result we feel able to control the Indriyas (the sense-organs, the nerve-centres). Thus alone will character be established, then alone a man gets to truth. Such a man is safe for ever; he cannot do any evil. You may place him in any company, there will be no danger for him.

There is a still higher state than having this good tendency, and that is the desire for liberation. You must remember that freedom of the soul is the goal of all Yogas, and each one equally leads to the same result.

By work alone men may get to where Buddha got largely by meditation or Christ by prayer. Buddha was a working Jnani, Christ was a Bhakta, but the same goal was reached by both of them.

The difficulty is here. Liberation means entire freedom — freedom from the bondage of good, as well as from the bondage of evil. A golden chain is as much a chain as an iron one. There is a thorn in my finger, and I use another to take the first one out; and when I have taken it out, I throw both of them aside; I have no necessity for keeping the second thorn, because both are thorns after all.

So the bad tendencies are to be counteracted by the good ones, and the bad impressions on the mind should be removed by the fresh waves of good ones, until all that is evil almost disappears, or is subdued and held in control in a corner of the mind; but after that, the good tendencies have also to be conquered. Thus the "attached" becomes the "unattached". Work, but let not the action or the thought produce a deep impression on the mind. Let the ripples come and go, let huge actions proceed from the muscles and the brain, but let them not make any deep impression on the soul.

How can this be done? We see that the impression of any action, to which we attach ourselves, remains. I may meet hundreds of persons during the day, and among them meet also one whom I love; and when I retire at night, I may try to think of all the faces I saw, but only that face comes before the mind — the face which I met perhaps only for one minute, and which I loved; all the others have vanished.

My attachment to this particular person caused a deeper impression on my mind than all the other faces. Physiologically the impressions have all been the same; every one of the faces that I saw pictured itself on the retina, and the brain took the pictures in, and yet there was no similarity of effect upon the mind. Most of the faces, perhaps, were entirely new faces, about which I had never thought before, but that one face of which I got only a glimpse found associations inside.

Perhaps I had pictured him in my mind for years, knew hundreds of things about him, and this one new vision of him awakened hundreds of sleeping memories in my mind; and this one impression having been repeated perhaps a hundred times more than those of the different faces together, will produce a great effect on the mind.

Therefore, be "unattached"; let things work; let brain centres work; work incessantly, but let not a ripple conquer the mind. Work as if you were a stranger in this land, a sojourner; work incessantly, but do not bind yourselves; bondage is terrible. This world is not our habitation, it is only one of the many stages through which we are passing.

Remember that great saying of the Sankhya, "The whole

of nature is for the soul, not the soul for nature." The very reason of nature's existence is for the education of the soul; it has no other meaning; it is there because the soul must have knowledge, and through knowledge free itself. If we remember this always, we shall never be attached to nature; we shall know that nature is a book in which we are to read, and that when we have gained the required knowledge, the book is of no more value to us.

Instead of that, however, we are identifying ourselves with nature; we are thinking that the soul is for nature, that the spirit is for the flesh, and, as the common saying has it, we think that man "lives to eat" and not "eats to live". We are continually making this mistake; we are regarding nature as ourselves and are becoming attached to it; and as soon as this attachment comes, there is the deep impression on the soul, which binds us down and makes us work not from freedom but like slaves.

The whole gist of this teaching is that you should work like a master and not as a slave; work incessantly, but do not do slave's work. Do you not see how everybody works? Nobody can be altogether at rest; ninety-nine per cent of mankind work like slaves, and the result is misery; it is all selfish work.

Work through freedom! Work through love! The word "love" is very difficult to understand; love never comes until there is freedom. There is no true love possible in the slave. If you buy a slave and tie him down in chains and make him work for you, he will work like a drudge, but there will be no love in him. So when we ourselves work for the things of the world as slaves, there can be no love in us, and our work is not true work.

This is true of work done for relatives and friends, and is true of work done for our own selves. Selfish work is slave's work; and here is a test. Every act of love brings happiness; there is no act of love which does not bring peace and blessedness as its reaction.

Real existence, real knowledge, and real love are eternally connected with one another, the three in one: where one of them is, the others also must be; they are the three aspects of the One without a second — the Existence - Knowledge - Bliss. When that existence becomes relative, we see it as the world; that knowledge becomes in its turn modified into the knowledge of the things of the world; and that bliss forms the foundation of all true love known to the heart of man.

Therefore true love can never react so as to cause pain either to the lover or to the beloved. Suppose a man loves a woman; he wishes to have her all to himself and feels extremely jealous about her every movement; he wants her to sit near him, to stand near him, and to eat and move at his bidding. He is a slave to her and wishes to have her as his slave.

That is not love; it is a kind of morbid affection of the slave, insinuating itself as love. It cannot be love, because it is painful; if she does not do what he wants, it brings him pain. With love there is no painful reaction; love only brings a reaction of bliss; if it does not, it is not love; it is mistaking something else for love. When you have succeeded in loving your husband, your wife, your children, the whole world, the universe, in such a manner that there is no reaction of pain or jealousy, no selfish feeling, then you are in a fit state to be unattached.

Krishna says, "Look at Me, Arjuna! If I stop from work for one moment, the whole universe will die. I have nothing to gain from work; I am the one Lord, but why do I work? Because I love the world."

God is unattached because He loves; that real love makes us unattached. Wherever there is attachment, the clinging to the things of the world, you must know that it is all physical attraction between sets of particles of matter — something that attracts two bodies nearer and nearer all the time and, if they cannot get near enough, produces pain; but where there is real love, it does not rest on physical attachment at all. Such lovers may be a thousand miles away from one another, but their love will be all the same; it does not die, and will never produce any painful reaction.

To attain this unattachment is almost a life-work, but as soon as we have reached this point, we have attained the goal of love and become free; the bondage of nature falls from us, and we see nature as she is; she forges no more chains for us; we stand entirely free and take not the results of work into consideration; who then cares for what the results may be?

Do you ask anything from your children in return for what you have given them? It is your duty to work for them, and there the matter ends. In whatever you do for a particular person, a city, or a state, assume the same attitude towards it as you have towards your children — expect nothing in return.

If you can invariably take the position of a giver, in which everything given by you is a free offering to the world, without any thought of return, then will your work bring you no attachment. Attachment comes only where we expect a return.

If working like slaves results in selfishness and attachment, working as master of our own mind gives rise to the bliss of non-attachment. We often talk of right and justice, but we find that in the world right and justice are mere baby's talk. There are two things which guide the conduct of men: might and mercy. The exercise of might is invariably the exercise of selfishness.

All men and women try to make the most of whatever power or advantage they have. Mercy is heaven itself;

to be good, we have all to be merciful. Even justice and right should stand on mercy. All thought of obtaining return for the work we do hinders our spiritual progress; nay, in the end it brings misery. There is another way in which this idea of mercy and selfless charity can be put into practice; that is, by looking upon work as "worship" in case we believe in a Personal God.

Here we give up all the fruits our work unto the Lord, and worshipping Him thus, we have no right to expect anything from mankind for the work we do. The Lord Himself works incessantly and is ever without attachment. Just as water cannot wet the lotus leaf, so work cannot bind the unselfish man by giving rise to attachment to results. The selfless and unattached man may live in the very heart of a crowded and sinful city; he will not be touched by sin.

Themes of the Gita: Attachment

Learn to help without pitying or feeling that there is any misery. Learn to be the same to enemy and to friend; then when you can do that and no longer have any desire, the goal is attained.

Cut down the banyan trcc of desire with the axe of non-attachment, and it will vanish utterly. It is all illusion. "He from whom blight and delusion have fallen, he who has conquered the evils of association, he alone is azad (free)."

To love anyone personally is bondage. Love all alike, then all desires fall off.

Time, the "eater of everything", comes, and all has to go. Why try to improve the earth, to paint the butterfly? It all has to go at last. Do not be mere white mice in a treadmill, working always and never accomplishing anything. Every desire is fraught with evil, whether the desire itself be good or evil. It is like a dog jumping for a piece of meat which is ever receding from his reach, and dying a dog's death at last. Do not be like that. Cut off all desire.

By thinking about sense objects, attachment to them is formed. From attachment comes longing, and longing breeds anger.

From anger comes delusion, and from delusion, confused memory. From confused memory comes the ruin of discrimination; and from the ruin of discrimination, a man perishes.

There is then no peace in the heart of a carnal man, nor in him that is addicted to outward things, but in the spiritual and devout man.

The Vedanta philosophy says that this whole universe — mental, physical, moral — is hypnotic. Who is the cause of this hypnotism? You yourself are to blame. This weeping and wailing and knocking your heads into corners against brick walls, as it were will not do you the least good.

However, knocking everything that is hypnotic on the head leads to what is called non-attachment; and clinging to more and more hypnotism is attachment. That is why in all religions you will find they wanted to give up the world, although many of them do not understand it.

There was a poor man who wanted some money; and somehow, he had heard that if he could get hold of a ghost, he might command him to bring money or anything else he liked; so he was very anxious to get hold of a ghost. At last he found a sage with great powers, and besought his help. The sage asked him what he would do with a ghost.

"I want a ghost to work for me; teach me how to get hold of one, sir; I desire it very much," replied the man.

But the sage said, "Don't disturb yourself, go home."

The next day the man went again to the sage and began to weep and pray, "Give me a ghost; I must have a ghost, sir, to help me."

At last the sage was disgusted, and said, "Take this charm, repeat this magic word, and a ghost will come, and whatever you say to him he will do. But beware; they are terrible beings, and must be kept continually busy. If you fail to give him work, he will take your life."

The man replied, "That is easy; I can give him work for all his life."

Then he went to a forest, and after long repetition of the magic word, a huge ghost appeared before him, and said, "I am a ghost. I have been conquered by your magic; but you must keep me constantly employed. The moment you fail to give me work I will kill you."

The man said, "Build me a palace," and the ghost said, "It is done; the palace is built." "

Bring me money," said the man. "Here is your money," said the ghost.

"Cut this forest down, and build a city in its place."

"That is done," said the ghost, "anything more?"

Now the man began to be frightened and thought he could give him nothing more to do; he did everything in a trice.

The ghost said, "Give me something to do or I will eat you up."

The poor man could find no further occupation for him, and was frightened. So he ran and ran and at last reached the sage, and said, "Oh, sir, protect my life!"

The sage said, "I will find you a way out. Look at that dog with a curly tail. Draw your sword quickly and cut the tail off and give it to the ghost to straighten out."

The man cut off the dog's tail and gave it to the ghost, saying, "Straighten that out for me."

The ghost took it and slowly and carefully straightened

it out, but as soon as he let it go, it instantly curled up again. Once more he laboriously straightened it out, only to find it again curled up as soon as he attempted to let go of it. Again he patiently straightened it out, but as soon as he let it go, it curled up again.

So he went on for days and days, until he was exhausted and said, "I was never in such trouble before in my life. I am an old veteran ghost, but never before was I in such trouble. I will make a compromise with you," he said to the man, "you let me off and I will let you keep all I have given you and will promise not to harm you."

The man was much pleased, and accepted the offer gladly.

This world is like a dog's curly tail, and people have been striving to straighten it out for hundreds of years; but when they let it go, it has curled up again. How could it be otherwise? One must first know how to work without attachment, then one will not be a fanatic.

When we know that this world is like a dog's curly tail and will never get straightened, we shall not become fanatics. If there were no fanaticism in the world, it would make much more progress than it does now.

It is a mistake to think that fanaticism can make for the

progress of mankind. On the contrary, it is a retarding element creating hatred and anger, and causing people to fight each other, and making them unsympathetic. We think that whatever we do or possess is the best in the world, and what we do not do or possess is of no value.

So, always remember the instance of the curly tail of the dog whenever you have a tendency to become a fanatic. You need not worry or make yourself sleepless about the world; it will go on without you.

When you have avoided fanaticism, then alone will you work well. It is the level-headed man, the calm man, of good judgment and cool nerves, of great sympathy and love, who does good work and so does good to himself. The fanatic is foolish and has no sympathy; he can never straighten the world, nor himself become pure and perfect.

Let us work without desire for name or fame or rule over others. Let us be free from the triple bonds of lust, greed of gain, and anger. And this truth is with us!

Was Krishna cunning? No, he was not cunning. He tried his best to prevent the war. It was Duryodhana who forced the war. But, when once in the thing, you should not recede — that is the man of duty. Do not run away, it is cowardice. When in the thing, you must do it. You should not budge an inch — of course not for a wrong thing; this war was a righteous war.

The devil comes in many guises — anger in the form of justice — passion in the form of duty. When it first comes, the man knows and then he forgets. Just as your pleaders' conscience; at first they know it is all Badmashi (roguery), then it is duty to their clients; at last they get hardened.

Leave off your commercial calculating ideas. If you can get rid of your attachment to a single thing, you are on the way to liberation.

Look at Krishna: he was great as a son, as a king, as a father, and all through his life he practiced the marvellous teachings which he preached." "He who in the midst of the greatest activity finds the sweetest peace, and in the midst of the greatest calmness is most active, he has known the secret of life."

Krishna shows the way how to do this — by being non-attached: do everything but do not get identified with anything. You are the soul, the pure, the free, all the time; you are the Witness. Our misery comes, not from work, but by our getting attached to something.

Take for instance, money: money is a great thing to have, earn it, says Krishna; struggle hard to get money, but don't get attached to it. So with children, with wife, husband, relatives, fame, everything; you have no need to shun them, only don't get attached.

There is only one attachment and that belongs to the Lord, and to none other. Work for them, love them, do good to them, sacrifice a hundred lives, if need be, for them, but never be attached. His own life was the exact exemplification of that.

We say that we cannot do good without at the same time doing some evil, or do evil without doing some good.

Knowing this, how can we work? There have, therefore, been sects in this world who have in an astoundingly preposterous way preached slow suicide as the only means to get out of the world, because if a man lives, he has to kill poor little animals and plants or do injury to something or some one. So according to them the only way out of the world is to die.

The Jains have preached this doctrine as their highest ideal. This teaching seems to be very logical. But the true solution is found in the Gita. It is the theory of non-attachment, to be attached to nothing while doing our work of life.

Know that you are separated entirely from the world, though you are in the world, and that whatever you may be doing in it, you are not doing that for your own sake. Any action that you do for yourself will bring its effect to bear upon you. If it is a good action, you will have to take the good effect, and if bad, you will have to take the bad effect; but any action that is not done for your own sake, whatever it be, will have no effect on you.

There is to be found a very expressive sentence in our scriptures embodying this idea: "Even if he kill the whole universe (or be himself killed), he is neither the killer nor the killed, when he knows that he is not acting for himself at all."

Therefore Karma-Yoga teaches, "Do not give up the world; live in the world, imbibe its influences as much as you can; but if it be for your own enjoyment's sake, work not at all."

Enjoyment should not be the goal. First kill your self and then take the whole world as yourself; as the old Christians used to say, "The old man must die." This old man is the selfish idea that the whole world is made for our enjoyment.

Foolish parents teach their children to pray, "O Lord, Thou hast created this sun for me and this moon for me," as if the Lord has had nothing else to do than to create everything for these babies.

Do not teach your children such nonsense. Then again, there are people who are foolish in another way: they teach us that all these animals were created for us to kill and eat, and that this universe is for the enjoyment of men. That is all foolishness.

A tiger may say, "Man was created for me," and pray, "O Lord, how wicked are these men who do not come and place themselves before me to be eaten; they are breaking Your law."

If the world is created for us, we are also created for the world. That this world is created for our enjoyment is the most wicked idea that holds us down. This world is not for our sake. Millions pass out of it every year; the world does not feel it; millions of others are supplied in their place. Just as much as the world is for us, so we also are for the world.

To work properly, therefore, you have first to give up the idea of attachment. Secondly, do not mix in the fray, hold yourself as a witness and go on working.

My master used to say, "Look upon your children as a nurse does." The nurse will take your baby and fondle it and play with it and behave towards it as gently as if it were her own child; but as soon as you give her notice to quit, she is ready to start off bag and baggage from the house. Everything in the shape of attachment is forgotten; it will not give the ordinary nurse the least pang to leave your children and take up other children.

Even so are you to be with all that you consider your own. You are the nurse, and if you believe in God, believe that all these things which you consider yours are really His. The greatest weakness often insinuates itself as the greatest good and strength. It is a weakness to think that any one is dependent on me, and that I can do good to another. This belief is the mother of all our attachment, and through this attachment comes all our pain.

We must inform our minds that no one in this universe depends upon us; not one beggar depends on our charity; not one soul on our kindness; not one living thing on our help. All are helped on by nature, and will be so helped even though millions of us were not here. The course of nature will not stop for such as you and me; it is, as already pointed out, only a blessed privilege to you and to me that we are allowed, in the way of helping others, to educate ourselves.

This is a great lesson to learn in life, and when we have learned it fully, we shall never be unhappy; we can go and mix without harm in society anywhere and everywhere. You may have wives and husbands, and regiments of servants, and kingdoms to govern; if only you act on the principle that the world is not for you and does not inevitably need you, they can do you no harm.

This very year some of your friends may have died. Is the world waiting without going on, for them to come again? Is its current stopped? No, it goes on. So drive out of your mind the idea that you have to do something for the world; the world does not require any help from you.

It is sheer nonsense on the part of any man to think that he is born to help the world; it is simply pride, it is selfishness insinuating itself in the form of virtue. When you have trained your mind and your nerves to realise this idea of the world's non-dependence on you or on anybody, there will then be no reaction in the form of pain resulting from work.

When you give something to a man and expect nothing — do not even expect the man to be grateful — his ingratitude will not tell upon you, because you never expected anything, never thought you had any right to anything in the way of a return. You gave him what he deserved; his own Karma got it for him; your Karma made you the carrier thereof.

Why should you be proud of having given away something? You are the porter that carried the money or other kind of gift, and the world deserved it by its own Karma. Where is then the reason for pride in you? There is nothing very great in what you give to the world.

When you have acquired the feeling of non-attachment, there will then be neither good nor evil for you. It is only selfishness that causes the difference between good and evil. It is a very hard thing to understand, but you will come to learn in time that nothing in the universe has power over you until you allow it to exercise such a power. Nothing has power over the Self of man, until the Self becomes a fool and loses independence.

So, by non-attachment, you overcome and deny the power of anything to act upon you. It is very easy to say that nothing has the right to act upon you until you allow it to do so; but what is the true sign of the man who really does not allow anything to work upon him, who is neither happy nor unhappy when acted upon by the external world? The sign is that good or ill fortune causes no change in his mind: in all conditions he continues to remain the same.

Themes of the Gita: the Atman

Between Brahman and the knower of Brahman there is not the least difference. " — He who knows the Brahman becomes the Brahman" (Mundaka, III. ii. 9).

The Atman cannot be known by the mind for It is Itself the Knower — this I have already said. Therefore man's relative knowledge reached up to the Avataras — those who are always established in the Atman. The highest ideal of Ishvara which the human mind can grasp is the Avatara. Beyond this there is no relative knowledge.

Such knowers of Brahman are rarely born in the world. And very few people can understand them. They alone are the proof of the truths of the scriptures — the towers of light in the ocean of the world. By the company of such Avataras and by their grace, the darkness of the mind disappears in a trice and realisation flashes immediately in the heart.

Why or by what process it comes cannot be ascertained. But it does come. I have seen it happen like that. Shri Krishna spoke the Gita, establishing Himself in the Atman. Those passages of the Gita where He speaks with the word "I", invariably indicate the Atman: "Take refuge in Me alone" means, "Be established in the Atman".

This knowledge of the Atman is the highest aim of the Gita. The references to Yoga etc. are but incidental to this realisation of the Atman. Those who have not this knowledge of the Atman are "suicides". "They kill themselves by the clinging to the unreal"; they lose their life in the noose of sense-pleasures.

You are also men, and can't you ignore this trash of sensual enjoyment that won't last for two days? Should you also swell the ranks of those who are born and die in utter ignorance? Accept the "beneficial" and discard the "pleasant".

Speak of this Atman to all, even to the lowest. By continued speaking your own intelligence also will clear up. And always repeat the great Mantras — " — Thou art That, " — I am That", " — All this is verily Brahman" — and have the courage of a lion in the heart.

What is there to fear? Fear is death — fear is the greatest sin. The human soul, represented by Arjuna, was touched with fear.

Therefore Bhagavan Shri Krishna, established in the Atman, spoke to him the teachings of the Gita. Still his fear would not leave him. Later, when Arjuna saw the Universal Form of the Lord, and became established in the Atman, then with all bondages of Karma burnt by the fire of knowledge, he fought the battle.

Themes of the Gita: Bhakti

Bhakti-Yoga is a real, genuine search after the Lord, a search beginning, continuing, and ending in love. One single moment of the madness of extreme love to God brings us eternal freedom.

"Bhakti", says Narada in his explanation of the Bhakti-aphorisms, "is intense love to God"; "When a man gets it, he loves all, hates none; he becomes satisfied for ever"; "This love cannot be reduced to any earthly benefit", because so long as worldly desires last, that kind of love does not come; "Bhakti is greater than karma, greater than Yoga, because these are intended for an object in view, while Bhakti is its own fruition, its own means and its own end."

Bhakti has been the one constant theme of our sages. Apart from the special writers on Bhakti, such as Shandilya or Narada, the great commentators on the Vyasa-Sutras , evidently advocates of knowledge (Jnana), have also something very suggestive to say about love. Even when the commentator is anxious to explain many, if not all, of the texts so as to make them import a sort of dry knowledge, the Sutras , in the chapter on worship especially, do not lend themselves to be easily manipulated in that fashion.

There is not really so much difference between knowledge (Jnana) and love (Bhakti) as people sometimes imagine. We shall see, as we go on, that in the end they converge and meet at the same point. So also is it with Raja-Yoga, which when pursued as a means to attain liberation, and not (as unfortunately it frequently becomes in the hands of charlatans and mystery-mongers) as an instrument to hoodwink the unwary, leads us also to the same goal.

The one great advantage of Bhakti is that it is the easiest and the most natural way to reach the great divine end in view; its great disadvantage is that in its lower forms it oftentimes degenerates into hideous fanaticism. The fanatical crew in Hinduism, or Mohammedanism, or Christianity, have always been almost exclusively recruited from these worshippers on the lower planes of Bhakti.

That singleness of attachment (Nishtha) to a loved object, without which no genuine love can grow, is very often also the cause of the denunciation of everything else. All the weak and undeveloped minds in every religion or country have only one way of loving their own ideal, i.e. by hating every other ideal. Herein is the explanation of why the same man who is so lovingly attached to his own ideal of God, so devoted to his own ideal of religion, becomes a howling fanatic as soon as he sees or hears anything of any other ideal.

This kind of love is somewhat like the canine instinct of guarding the master's property from intrusion; only, the instinct of the dog is better than the reason of man, for the dog never mistakes its master for an enemy in whatever dress he may come before it. Again, the fanatic loses all power of judgment.

Personal considerations are in his case of such absorbing interest that to him it is no question at all what a man says — whether it is right or wrong; but the one thing he is always particularly careful to know is who says it. The same man who is kind, good, honest, and loving to people of his own opinion, will not hesitate to do the vilest deeds when they are directed against persons beyond the pale of his own religious brotherhood.

But this danger exists only in that stage of Bhakti which is called thepreparatory (Gauni). When Bhakti has become ripe and has passed into that form which is called the supreme (Para), no more is there any fear of these hideous manifestations of fanaticism; that soul which is overpowered by this higher form of Bhakti is too near the God of Love to become an instrument for the diffusion of hatred.

It is not given to all of us to be harmonious in the building up of our characters in this life: yet we know that that character is of the noblest type in which all these three — knowledge and love and Yoga — are harmoniously fused. Three things are necessary for a bird to fly — the two wings and the tail as a rudder for steering.

Jnana (Knowledge) is the one wing, Bhakti (Love) is

the other, and Yoga is the tail that keeps up the balance. For those who cannot pursue all these three forms of worship together in harmony and take up, therefore, Bhakti alone as their way, it is necessary always to remember that forms and ceremonials, though absolutely necessary for the progressive soul, have no other value than taking us on to that state in which we feel the most intense love to God.

There is a little difference in opinion between the teachers of knowledge and those of love, though both admit the power of Bhakti. The Jnanis hold Bhakti to be an instrument of liberation, the Bhaktas look upon it both as the instrument and the thing to be attained.

To my mind this is a distinction without much difference. In fact, Bhakti, when used as an instrument, really means a lower form of worship, and the higher form becomes inseparable from the lower form of realisation at a later stage. Each seems to lay a great stress upon his own peculiar method of worship, forgetting that with perfect love true knowledge is bound to come even unsought, and that from perfect knowledge true love is inseparable.

Bearing this in mind let us try to understand what the great Vedantic commentators have to say on the subject.

In explaining the Sutra Avrittirasakridupadeshat

(Meditation is necessary, that having been often enjoined.), Bhagavan Shankara says, "Thus people say, 'He is devoted to the king, he is devoted to the Guru'; they say this of him who follows his Guru, and does so, having that following as the one end in view. Similarly they say, 'The loving wife meditates on her loving husband'; here also a kind of eager and continuous remembrance is meant." This is devotion according to Shankara.

Meditation again is a constant remembrance (of the thing meditated upon) flowing like an unbroken stream of oil poured out from one vessel to another. When this kind of remembering has been attained (in relation to God) all bondages break.

Thus it is spoken of in the scriptures regarding constant remembering as a means to liberation. This remembering again is of the same form as seeing, because it is of the same meaning as in the passage, 'When He who is far and near is seen, the bonds of the heart are broken, all doubts vanish, and all effects of work disappear.'

He who is near can be seen, but he who is far can only be remembered. Nevertheless the scripture says that he have to see Him who is near as well as Him who, is far, thereby indicating to us that the above kind of remembering is as good as seeing.

This remembrance when exalted assumes the same form as seeing. Worship is constant remembering as may be seen from the essential texts of scriptures. Knowing, which is the same as repeated worship, has been described as constant remembering.

Thus the memory, which has attained to the height of what is as good as direct perception, is spoken of in the Shruti as a means of liberation. 'This Atman is not to be reached through various sciences, nor by intellect, nor by much study of the Vedas. Whomsoever this Atman desires, by him is the Atman attained, unto him this Atman discovers Himself.'

Here, after saying that mere hearing, thinking and meditating are not the means of attaining this Atman, it is said, 'Whom this Atman desires, by him the Atman is attained.'

The extremely beloved is desired; by whomsoever this Atman is extremely beloved, he becomes the most beloved of the Atman. So that this beloved may attain the Atman, the Lord Himself helps. For it has been said by the Lord: 'Those who are constantly attached to Me and worship Me with love — I give that direction to their will by which they come to Me.'

Therefore it is said that, to whomsoever this remembering, which is of the same form as direct perception, is very dear, because it is dear to the Object of such memory perception, he is desired by the Supreme Atman, by him the Supreme Atman is attained. This constant remembrance is denoted by the word Bhakti.

(So says Bhagavan Ramanuja in his commentary on the Sutra Athato Brahma-jijnasa.)

In commenting on the Sutra of Patanjali, Ishvara pranidhanadva, i.e. "Or by the worship of the Supreme Lord" — Bhoja says, "Pranidhana is that sort of Bhakti in which, without seeking results, such as sense-enjoyments etc., all works are dedicated to that Teacher of teachers."

Bhagavan Vyasa also, when commenting on the same, defines Pranidhana as "the form of Bhakti by which the mercy of the Supreme Lord comes to the Yogi, and blesses him by granting him his desires". According to Shandilya, "Bhakti is intense love to God."

The best definition is, however, that given by the king of Bhaktas, Prahlada:

"That deathless love which the ignorant have for the fleeting objects of the senses — as I keep meditating on Thee — may not that love slip away from my heart!" Love ! For whom? For the Supreme Lord Ishvara.

Love for any other being, however great cannot be Bhakti; for, as Ramanuja says in his Shri Bhashya, quoting an ancient Acharya, i.e. a great teacher:

"From Brahma to a clump of grass, all things that live in the world are slaves of birth and death caused by Karma; therefore they cannot be helpful as objects of meditation, because they are all in ignorance and subject to change."

In commenting on the word Anurakti used by Shandilya, the commentator Svapneshvara says that it means Anu, after, and Rakti, attachment; i.e. the attachment which comes after the knowledge of the nature and glory of God; else a blind attachment to any one, e.g. to wife or children, would be Bhakti.

We plainly see, therefore, that Bhakti is a series or succession of mental efforts at religious realisation beginning with ordinary worship and ending in a supreme intensity of love for Ishvara.

Bhagavan Ramakrishna used to tell a story of some men who went into a mango orchard and busied themselves in counting the leaves, the twigs, and the branches, examining their colour, comparing their size, and noting down everything most carefully, and then got up a learned discussion on each of these topics, which were undoubtedly highly interesting to them. But one of them, more sensible than the others, did not care for all these things. and instead thereof, began to eat the mango fruit. And was he not wise?

So leave this counting of leaves and twigs and note-taking to others. This kind of work has its proper place, but not here in the spiritual domain. You never see a strong spiritual man among these "leaf counters".

Religion, the highest aim, the highest glory of man, does not require so much labour. If you want to be a Bhakta, it is not at all necessary for you to know whether Krishna was born in Mathura or in Vraja, what he was doing, or just the exact date on which he pronounced the teachings of the Gita.

You only require to feel the craving for the beautiful lessons of duty and love in the Gita. All the other particulars about it and its author are for the enjoyment of the learned. Let them have what they desire. Say "Shantih, Shantih" to their learned controversies, and let us "eat the mangoes".

To obtain Bhakti, seek the company of holy men who have Bhakti, and read books like the Gita and the Imitation of Christ; always think of the attributes of God.

Thoughts on the Gita

Read the Gita and the Sutras of Vyasa, or get someone to read them to you. In the Gita the way is laid open to all men and women, to all caste and colour, but Vyasa tries to put meanings upon the Vedas to cheat the poor Shudras. Is God a nervous fool like you that the flow of His river of mercy would be dammed up by a piece of meat? If such be He, His value is not a pie!

The less you read, the better. Read the Gita and other good works on Vedanta. That is all you need. The present system of education is all wrong. The mind is crammed with facts before it knows how to think. Control of the mind should be taught first. If I had my education to get over again and had any voice in the matter, I would learn to master my mind first, and then gather facts if I wanted them. It takes people a long time to learn things because they can't concentrate their minds at will.

"Spirituality can never be attained until materiality is gone."

The first discourse in the Gita can be taken allegorically.

"The Vedas only teach of things in nature, only teach of nature."

We are always letting sentiment usurp the place of duty, and flattering ourselves that we are acting in response to true love.

We must get beyond emotionalism if we would be able to renounce. Emotion belongs to the animals. They are creatures of emotion entirely.

The Bhagavad-Gita is the best commentary we have on the Vedanta philosophy. Curiously enough the scene is laid on the battlefield, where Krishna teaches this philosophy to Arjuna; and the doctrine which stands out luminously in every page of the Gita is intense activity, but in the midst of it, eternal calmness.

This is the secret of work, to attain which is the goal of the Vedanta. Inactivity, as we understand it in the sense of passivity, certainly cannot be the goal. Were it so, then the walls around us would be the most intelligent; they are inactive. Clods of earth, stumps of trees, would be the greatest sages in the world; they are inactive.

Nor does inactivity become activity when it is combined with passion. Real activity, which is the goal of Vedanta, is combined with eternal calmness, the calmness which cannot be ruffled, the balance of mind which is never disturbed, whatever happens. And we all know from our experience in life that that is the best attitude for work.

Ancient India had for centuries been the battlefield for the ambitious projects of two of her foremost classes — the Brahmins and the Kshatriyas.

On the one hand, the priesthood stood between the lawless social tyranny of the princes over the masses whom the Kshatriyas declared to be their legal food. On the other hand, the Kshatriya power was the one potent force which struggled with any success against the spiritual tyranny of the priesthood and the ever-increasing chain of ceremonials which they were forging to bind down the people with.

The tug of war began in the earliest periods of the history of our race, and throughout the Shrutis it can be distinctly traced. A momentary lull came when Shri Krishna, leading the faction of Kshatriya power and of Jnana, showed the way to reconciliation. The result was the teachings of the Gita — the essence of philosophy, of liberality, of religion.

The result of every work is mixed with good and evil. There is no good work that has not a touch of evil in it. Like smoke round the fire, some evil always clings to work. We should engage in such works as bring the largest amount of good and the smallest measure of evil.

Arjuna killed Bhishma and Drona; if this had not been

done Duryodhana could not have been conquered, the force of evil would have triumphed over the force of good, and thus a great calamity would have fallen on the country. The government of the country would have been usurped by a body of proud unrighteous kings, to the great misfortune of the people.

Similarly, Shri Krishna killed Kamsa, Jarasandha, and others who were tyrants, but not a single one of his deeds was done for himself. Every one of them was for the good of others. We are reading the Gita by candle-light, but numbers of insects are being burnt to death.

Thus it is seen that some evil clings to work. Those who work without any consciousness of their lower ego are not affected with evil, for they work for the good of the world. To work without motive, to work unattached, brings the highest bliss and freedom. This secret of Karma-Yoga is taught by the Lord Shri Krishna in the Gita.

"The Gita says that there are three kinds of charity: the Tamasic, the Rajasic and the Sattvic. Tamasic charity is performed on an impulse. It is always making mistakes. The doer thinks of nothing but his own impulse to be kind. Rajasic charity is what a man does for his own glory. And Sattvic charity is that which is given to the right person, in the right way, and at the proper time. . . .

"When it comes to the Sattvic, I think more and more of a certain great Western woman in whom I have seen that quiet giving, always to the right person in the right way, at the right time, and never making a mistake.

"For my own part, I have been learning that even charity can go too far. . . .

"As I grow older I find that I look more and more for greatness in little things. I want to know what a great man eats and wears, and how he speaks to his servants. I want to find a Sir Philip Sidney 352 greatness! Few men would remember the thirst of others, even in the moment of death.

"But anyone will be great in a great position! Even the coward will grow brave in the glare of the footlights. The world looks on. Whose heart will not throb? Whose pulse will not quicken till he can do his best?

"More and more the true greatness seems to me that of the worm doing its duty silently, steadily, from moment to moment and from hour to hour." (CWSN 1: 137)

Jnana is taught very clearly by Krishna in the Bhagavad-Gita. This great poem is held to be the Crown jewel of all Indian literature. It is a kind of commentary on the Vedas. It shows us that our battle for spirituality must be fought out in this life; so we must not flee from it, but rather compel it to give us all that it holds.

As the Gita typifies this struggle for higher things, it is highly poetical to lay the scene in a battlefield. Krishna in the guise of a charioteer to Arjuna, leader of one of the opposing armies, urges him not to be sorrowful, not to fear death, since he knows he is immortal, that nothing which changes can be in the real nature of man.

Through chapter after chapter, Krishna teaches the higher truths of philosophy and religion to Arjuna. It is these teachings which make this poem so wonderful; practically the whole of the Vedanta philosophy is included in them.

The Vedas teach that the soul is infinite and in no way affected by the death of the body. The soul is a circle whose circumference is nowhere, but whose centre is in some body. Death (so-called) is but a change of centre. God is a circle whose circumference is nowhere and whose centre is everywhere, and when we can get out of the narrow centre of body, we shall realise God — our true Self.

The present is only a line of demarcation between the past and the future; so we cannot rationally say that we care only for the present, as it has no existence apart from the past and the future. It is all one complete whole, the idea of time being merely a condition imposed upon us by the form of our understanding.

Shlokas and Their Meanings

I

क्लैब्यं मा स्म गमः पार्थ नैतत्त्वय्युपपद्यते |

क्षुद्रं हृदयदौर्बल्यं त्यक्त्वोत्तिष्ठ परन्तप || 3||

klaibyaṁ mā sma gamaḥ pārtha naitat
tvayyupapadyate

kṣhudraṁ hṛidaya-daurbalyaṁ tyaktvottiṣhṭha
parantapa

Translation:

O Arjuna! Do not yield to impotence. It does not befit you. Cast off this wretched weakness of heart. Arise, O scorcher of enemies!

Swami Vivekananda says, "“Yield not to unmanliness, O son of Pritha! Ill doth it befit thee. Cast off this mean faint-heartedness and arise, O scorcher of thine enemies.” … In these and similar passages in the Gita the Lord is showing the way to dharma.

"For all of us in this world life is a continuous fight. … Many a time comes when we want to interpret our weakness and cowardice as forgiveness and renunciation. There is no merit in the renunciation of a beggar. If a person who can give a blow forbears, there is merit in that. If a person who has, gives up, there is merit in that.

"We know how often in our lives through laziness and cowardice we give up the battle and try to hypnotize our minds into the belief that we are brave. The Gita opens with this very significant verse: "Arise, O Prince! Give up this faint-heartedness, this weakness! Stand up and fight!"

"Then Arjuna, trying to argue the matter with Krishna, brings higher moral ideas, how non-resistance is better than resistance, and so on. He is trying to justify himself, but he cannot fool Krishna. Krishna is the higher Self, or God. He sees through the argument at once. In this case the motive is weakness. Arjuna sees his own relatives and he cannot strike them. …

"There is a conflict in Arjuna's heart between his emotionalism and his duty. The nearer we are to beasts and birds, the more we are in the hells of emotion. We call it love. It is self-hypnotization. We are under the control of our emotions like animals. A cow can sacrifice its life for its young. Every animal can. What of that? It is not the blind, birdlike emotion that leads to perfection.

To reach the eternal consciousness, that is the goal of man! There emotion has no place, nor sentimentalism, nor anything that belongs to the senses — only the light of pure reason. There man stands as spirit."

In reading the Bhagavad Gita, many of you in Western countries may have felt astonished at the second chapter, wherein Shri Krishna calls Arjuna a hypocrite and a coward because of his refusal to fight, or offer resistance, on account of his adversaries being his friends and relatives, making the plea that non-resistance was the highest ideal of love.

This is a great lesson for us all to learn, that in all matters the two extremes are alike. The extreme positive and the extreme negative are always similar. When the vibrations of light are too slow, we do not see them, nor do we see them when they are too rapid. So with sound; when very low in pitch, we do not hear it; when very high, we do not hear it either.

Of like nature is the difference between resistance and non-resistance. One man does not resist because he is weak, lazy, and cannot, not because he will not; the other man knows that he can strike an irresistible blow if he likes; yet he not only docs not strike, but blesses his enemies. The one who from weakness resists not commits a sin, and as such cannot receive any benefit from the non-resistance; while the other would commit a sin by offering resistance. Buddha gave up his throne and renounced his position, that was true renunciation; but there cannot be any question of renunciation in the case of a beggar who has nothing to renounce.

So we must always be careful about what we really mean when we speak of this non-resistance and ideal love. We must first take care to understand whether we have the power of resistance or not. Then, having the power, if we renounce it and do not resist, we are doing a grand act of love; but if we cannot resist, and yet, at the same time, try to deceive ourselves into the belief that we are actuated by motives of the highest love, we are doing the exact opposite.

Arjuna became a coward at the sight of the mighty array against him; his "love" made him forget his duty towards his country and king. That is why Shri Krishna told him that he was a hypocrite: Thou talkest like a wise man, but thy actions betray thee to be a coward; therefore stand up and fight!

And mark you, those things which you see in pusillanimous, effeminate folk who speak in a nasal tone chewing every syllable, whose voice is as thin as of one who has been starving for a week, who are like a tattered wet rag, who never protest or are moved even if kicked by anybody — those are the signs of the lowest tamas, those are the signs of death, not of sattva — all corruption and stench. It is because Arjuna was going to fall into the ranks of these men that the Lord is explaining matters to him so elaborately in the Gita. Is that not the fact?

II

न त्वेवाहं जातु नासं न त्वं नेमे जनाधपिा |

न चैव न भवष्यिामः सर्वे वयमतः परम् || 12||

na tvevāhaṁ jātu nāsaṁ na tvaṁ neme janādhipāḥ

na chaiva na bhavişhyāmaḥ sarve vayamataḥ param

Translation:

Never was there a time when I did not exist, nor you, nor these kings of men. Never will there be a time hereafter when any of us shall cease to be.

"You cannot die nor can I. There was never a time when we did not exist. There will never be a time when we shall not exist.

"People talk about the beginning of the world, the beginning of man. The word beginning simply means the beginning of the cycle. It nowhere means the beginning of the whole Cosmos. It is impossible that creation could have a beginning. No one of you can imagine a time of beginning. That which has a beginning must have an end. "Never did I not exist, nor you, nor will any of us ever hereafter cease to be," says the Bhagavad Gita. Wherever the beginning of creation is mentioned, it means the beginning of a cycle. Your body will meet with death, but your soul, never."

III

य एनं वेत्त्ति हन्तारं यश्चैनं मन्यते हतम् |

उभौ तौ न वजिानीतो नायं हन्त्ति न हन्यते || 19||

ya enaṁ vetti hantāraṁ yaśh chainaṁ manyate hatam

ubhau tau na vijānīto nāyaṁ hanti na hanyate

Translation:

He who thinks that Atma slays, or he who thinks that Atma is Slain, both these do not know the Truth. Atma does not slay, nor is slain.

Any action that you do for yourself will bring its effect to bear upon you. If it is a good action, you will have to take the good effect, and if bad, you will have to take the bad effect; but any action that is not done for your own sake, whatever it be, will have no effect on you.

"There is to be found a very expressive sentence in our scriptures embodying this idea: "Even if he kills the whole universe (or be himself killed), he is neither the killer nor the killed, when he knows that he is not acting for himself at all." Therefore karma-yoga teaches, "Do not give up the world; live in the world, imbibe its influences as much as you can; but if it be for your own enjoyment's sake, work not at all." Enjoyment should not be the goal."

IV

न जायते म्रयिते वा कदार्चा

नायं भूत्वा भवतिा वा न भूय: |

अजो नति्य: शाश्वतोऽयं पुराणो

न हन्यते हन्यमाने शरीरे || 20||

na jāyate mriyate vā kadāchin

nāyaṁ bhūtvā bhavitā vā na bhūyaḥ

ajo nityaḥ śhāśhvato ’yaṁ purāṇo

na hanyate hanyamāne śharīre

Translation:

Atma is not born, nor does it ever die; after having been it does not cease to be, unborn, eternal, changeless and ancient, it is not killed when the body is destroyed.

Now freedom is only possible when no external power can exert any influence, produce any change. Freedom is only possible to the being who is beyond all conditions, all laws, all bondages of cause and effect. In other words, the unchangeable alone can be free and, therefore, immortal. This Being, this Atman, this real Self of man, the free, the unchangeable is beyond all conditions, and as such, it has neither birth nor death. 'Without birth or death, eternal, ever-existing is this soul of man.

V

वासांसि जीर्णानि यथा विहाय

नवानि गृह्णाति नरोऽपराणि।

तथा शरीराणि विहाय जीर्णा

न्यन्यानि संयाति नवानि देही ||22||

vāsānsi jīrṇāni yathā vihāya

navāni gṛihṇāti naro 'parāṇi

tathā śharīrāṇi vihāya jīrṇānya

nyāni sanyāti navāni dehī

Translation:

Just as a man casts off his worn-out clothes and puts on new ones so also the Self throws away its worn-out bodies and takes other fresh bodies.

So far we have discussed God and nature, eternal God and eternal nature. What about souls? They also are eternal. No soul was ever created; neither can the soul die. Nobody can even imagine his own death. The soul is infinite, eternal. How can it die? It changes bodies. As a man takes off his old, worn-out garments and puts on new and fresh ones, even so the worn-out body is thrown away and a fresh body is taken.

There are two sorts of races, the divine and the demonic. The divine think that they are soul and spirit. The demonic think that they are bodies. The old Indian philosophers tried to insist that the body is nothing. 'As a man emits his old garment and takes a new one, even so the old body is shed and he takes a new one.'

VI

आश्चर्यवत्पश्यति कश्चिदेन

माश्चर्यवद्वदति तथैव चान्यः |

आश्चर्यवच्चैनमन्यः शृणोति

श्रुत्वाप्येनं वेद न चैव कश्चित् || 29||

āśhcharya-vat paśhyati kaśhchid enan

āśhcharya-vad vadati tathaiva chānyaḥ

āśhcharya-vach chainam anyaḥ śhṛiṇoti

śhrutvāpyenaṁ veda na chaiva kaśhchit

Translation:

Some look on the Self as a wonder; some speak of It as a wonder; some hear of It as a wonder; still others, though hearing, do not understand It at all.

Some look at It the Self with wonder. Some talk of It as wonderful. Others hear of It as wonderful. Others, hearing of It, do not understand.

In the Ramakrishna Incarnation there is knowledge, devotion and love — infinite knowledge, infinite love, infinite work, infinite compassion for all beings. You have not yet been able to understand him. **"शरुत्वाप्येनं वेद न चैव कश्चित्** — Even after hearing about Him, most people do not understand Him." What the whole Hindu race has thought in ages, he lived in one life. His life is the living commentary to the Vedas of all nations. People will come to know him by degrees.

VII

सुखदु:खे समे कृत्वा लाभालाभौ जयाजयौ |

ततो युद्धाय युज्यस्व नैवं पापमवाप्स्यसि || 38||

sukha-duḥkhe same kṛitvā lābhālābhau jayājayau

tato yuddhāya yujyasva naivaṁ pāpam avāpsyasi

Translation:

Having an equal mind in pain and pleasure, gain and loss, victory and defeat, engage in battle and thereby you will not incur sin.

Making pleasure and misery the same, making success and defeat the same, do thou stand up and fight.

When I became a sannyasin, I consciously took the step, knowing that this body would have to die of starvation. What of that, I am a beggar. My friends are poor, I love the poor, I welcome poverty. I am glad that I sometimes have to starve. I ask help of none. What is the use? Truth will preach itself, it will not die for the want of the helping hands of me! "Making happiness and misery the same, making success and failure the same, fight thou on." It is that eternal love, unruffled equanimity under all circumstances, and perfect freedom from jealousy or animosity that will tell. That will tell, nothing else.

VIII

बुद्धयियुक्तो जहातीह उभे सुकृतदुष्कृते |

तस्माद्योगाय युज्यस्व योगः कर्मसु कौशलम् || 50||

buddhi-yukto jahātīha ubhe sukṛita-duṣhkṛite

tasmād yogāya yujyasva yogaḥ karmasu kauśhalam

Translation:

The man of equanimity born of wisdom releases himself both from good and bad even in this life. Therefore strive for nishkama karma with an equal mind. Yoga is skill in action.

Our karma determines what we deserve and what we can assimilate. We are responsible for what we are; and whatever we wish ourselves to be, we have the power to make ourselves. If what we are now has been the result of our own past actions, it certainly follows that whatever we wish to be in future can be produced by our present actions; so we have to know how to act.

You will say, "What is the use of learning how to work? Everyone works in some way or other in this world." But there is such a thing as frittering away our energies. With regard to karma-yoga, the Gita says that it is doing work with cleverness and as a science; by knowing how to work, one can obtain the greatest results."

IX

श्रुतविप्रितपिन्ना ते यदा स्थास्यती निश्चला |

समाधावचला बुद्धसि्तदा योगमवाप्स्यसि || 53||

śhruti-vipratipannā te yadā sthāsyati niśhchalā

samādhāv-achalā buddhis tadā yogam avāpsyasi

Translation:

When your intellect which is perplexed by hearing the various sastras becomes steady and immovable in ecstatic concentration, then you shall attain union with the Supreme Being.

Who can work without any attachment? That is the real question. Such a man is the same whether his work succeeds or fails. His heart does not give one false beat even if his whole life-work is burnt to ashes in a moment. "This is the sage who always works for work's sake without caring for the results. Thus he goes beyond the pain of birth and death. Thus he becomes free." Then he sees that this attachment is all delusion. The Self can never be attached. ... Then he goes beyond all the scriptures and philosophies.

If the mind is deluded and pulled into a whirlpool by books and scriptures, what is the good of all these scriptures? One says this, another says that. What book shall you take? Stand alone! See the glory of your own soul, and see that you will have to work. Then you will become a man of firm will.

The only way to understand Him and the universe is to go beyond reason, beyond consciousness. 'When thou goest beyond the heard and the hearing, the thought and the thinking, then alone wilt thou come to Truth.'

X

दुःखेष्वनुद्विग्नमनाः सुखेषु विगतस्पृहः ।

वीतरागभयक्रोधः स्थितधीर्मुनिरुच्यते || 56||

duḥkheṣhv-anudvigna-manāḥ sukheṣhu vigata-spṛihaḥ

vīta-rāga-bhaya-krodhaḥ sthita-dhīr munir uchyate

Translation:

He whose mind is not troubled in sorrow, who does not hanker after pleasures and is free from attachment fear and hatred, is called the sage of steady wisdom.

Arjuna asks: "Who is a person of established will?" Krishna answers: "The man who has given up all desires, who desires nothing, not even this life, nor freedom, nor gods, nor work, nor anything. When he has become perfectly satisfied, he has no more cravings." He has seen the glory of the Self and has found that the world, and the gods, and heaven are … within his own Self. Then the gods become no gods; death becomes no death; life becomes no life. Everything has changed. "A man is said to be illumined if his will has become firm, if his mind is not disturbed by misery, if he does not desire any happiness, if he is free of all attachment, of all fear, of all anger.

XI

आपूर्यमाणमचलप्रतिष्ठं

समुद्रमापः प्रविशन्ति यद्वत् ।

तद्वत्कामा यं प्रविशन्ति सर्वे

स शान्तिमाप्नोति न कामकामी || 70||

āpūryamāṇam achala-pratiṣhṭhaṁ

samudram āpaḥ praviśhanti yadvat

tadvat kāmā yaṁ praviśhanti sarve

sa śhāntim āpnoti na kāma-kāmī

Translation:

As the ocean is filled with water flowing into it from all sides and remains immovable, so the man into whom all desires flow, but is not a bit affected attains peace and not the man who craves the desires.

As all the rivers of the world constantly pour their waters into the ocean, but the ocean's grand, majestic nature remains undisturbed and unchanged, so even though all the senses bring in sensations from nature, the ocean-like heart of the sage knows no disturbance, knows no fear. Let miseries come in millions of rivers and happiness in hundreds! I am no slave to misery! I am no slave to happiness!

The mission of the Institute of Thought and Philosophy is to preserve and propagate the teachings of Swami Vivekananda. This great Indian spiritual leader is known for introducing the West to Hinduism. Drawing from his vast literary legacy, we provide valuable insights and practical guidance for modern living.

Have any query or feedback? Please reach out to us at
ITPPress123@gmail.com